Celebrating
GIRLS

Celebrating GIRLS

...

Nurturing and Empowering Our Daughters

Virginia Beane Rutter

CONARI PRESS
Berkeley, CA

For information, contact Conari Press, 2550 Ninth St.,
Suite 101, Berkeley, CA 94710.

Conari Press books are distributed by Publishers Group West

Charlotte Johnson Frisbie's "A Study of the Navajo Girl's Puberty
Ceremony" from Kinaabla © 1967, Wesleyan University Press
by permission University Press of New England.

From *The Dead and The Living* by Sharon Olds. Copyright © 1983 by
Sharon Olds. Reprinted by permission of Alfred A. Knopf Inc.

Cover design: Suzanne Albertson
Cover photo: Jennifer Braham, Berkeley, California
Author photo: Photography by Vera, Mill Valley, California
Special thanks to cover models: Cristine A.Tennant, Meagan Alderson,
Anna Darby, Natalia Casella, and Alice Walton

ISBN: 1-57432-053-2

Library of Congress Cataloging-in-Publication Data

Rutter, Virginia Beane.
Celebrating Girls : nurturing and empowering our
daughters /Virginia Beane Rutter.
        p.   cm.
Includes bibliographical references and resource guide.
ISBN 1-57432-053-2
1. Girls. 2. Mothers and Daughters. 3. Self-esteem in children.
4. Femininity (Psychology) 5. Rites and ceremonies. I. Title
HQ777.R87   1996   96-7851
306.874´3—dc20   CIP

for Melina Centomani Rutter

Contents

■ ■ ■

Bread

When my daughter makes bread, a cloud of flour
hangs in the air like pollen. She sifts and
sifts again, the salt and sugar
close as the grain of her skin. She heats the
water to body temperature
with the sausage lard, fragrant as her scalp
the day before hair-wash, and works them together on a
floured board. Her broad palms
bend the paste toward her and the heel of her hand
presses it away, until the dough
begins to snap, glossy and elastic as the
torso bending over it,
this ten-year-old girl, random specks of
yeast in her flesh beginning to heat,
her volume doubling every month now, but still
raw and hard. She slaps the dough and it
crackles under her palm, sleek and
ferocious and still leashed, like her body, no
breasts rising like bubbles of air toward the
surface of the loaf. She greases the pan, she is
shaped, glazed, and at any moment goes
into the oven, to turn to that porous
warm substance, and then under the
knife to be sliced for the having, the tasting, and the
giving of life.

—Sharon Olds

Acknowledgments
■ ■ ■

Thank you, thank you to the mothers and daughters, aunts, cousins, grandmothers, and "big sisters," who offered their stories for celebrating girls all over the world: Alice Abarbanel, Jennifer Barker, Jessica Barker, Rebecca Barker, Jan Berry-Kadrie, Pam Bleier, Andrea Blum, Eda Cole, Meinrad Craighead, Dorothy Cribbs, Jennifer Cribbs, Justine Beane Cunningham, Jessica Curiale, JoAnne Dellaverson, Maureen Denicke, Jyoti Elias, Anjuli Elias, Sue Nathanson Elkind, Annie Hagbom, Eva Leveton, Anandi Matteson, Holly Powell, Jeannette Sears, Natalie Sears, Nancy Spring, Sarah Swanger, Dorothy Taber, Lynn Taber-Borcherdt, Frances Zavala Tobriner, Nancy Tracy, Sara Van Acker, Judith Ward, Linda Cutts Weintraub, Sarah Weintraub, Catherine White, Barbara Young, and all the other women and girls behind the scenes who have contributed to my knowledge of girls.

My agent, Barbara Moulton, deserves particular tribute for taking on this project as a labor of love and seeing it through to publication. Thanks also to Mary Jane Ryan of Conari Press who, with her vision and enthusiasm, suggested widening the scope of *Celebrating Girls* and energetically edited the manuscript.

My boundless gratitude to my mother, Justine Beane Cunningham, and friends Jan Berry-Kadrie and Lynn Taber-Borcherdt—the three graces who renewed my flagging spirit at key moments in the writing and offered editorial comments as needed. And to Isabel Allende who generously blessed the book with her fine endorsement.

Celebrating Girls could never have been written without my wonderful daughter, to whom it is dedicated. And, finally, my love to my son, Naftali, and to my husband, Peter—the men in my life—whose solid support, as always, sustained me.

ONE

■ ■ ■

Celebrating Girls

THE WORD *CELEBRATE* comes from the ancient Greek word *melpo*—meaning to sing, to dance, to praise! I offer this book in praise of girls, to help nurture and empower them. It addresses the question of what we can do to enhance our daughters' feminine self-worth.

Thanks to groundbreaking books such as In a Different Voice by Carol Gilligan and Reviving Ophelia: Saving the Selves of Adolescent Girls by Mary Pipher, we are all aware of the severe pressures and dangers

1

that diminish girls' self-esteem as they approach adolescence. Girls who are free-thinking and expressive, who speak their minds and their hearts, suddenly begin to lose their voices and become silent. They reject their individuality for a cultural norm about the way girls "should" look ("thin") and behave ("good"). As Peggy Orenstein concluded in *Schoolgirls: Young Women, Self-Esteem and the Confidence Gap*, girls still view their gender as a liability. "By sixth grade, it is clear that both girls and boys have learned to equate maleness with opportunity and femininity with constraint." In short, girls begin early in life to stop believing in themselves.

As concerned mothers, we read all this depressing news and wonder if there is anything we can do about it. I believe the answer is a decided yes: Mothers and other adult women in girls' lives can raise girls with vital, intact feminine spirits through cherishing care and healthy challenges celebrated in meaningful ways. Anything that we do to enhance the self-esteem of a girl in our lives will have positive consequences toward increasing the self-esteem of other girls and women. As Gloria Steinem once said, "Women's history is about human beings, women and men, and for all days. But even one month of looking at the world as if women *mattered* can change the rest of your life."

Affirming femininity can be done as a natural extension of the normal things we do every day with and for our daughters. Nurturing and empowering our daughters begins with celebrating her female body from birth. The earliest intimacies—bathing, hairwashing, and haircombing—are opportunities to give a young girl the valued sense of herself that she needs to counteract the negative messages she will receive her whole life about being female. These elements from everyday life that are part of most girls' initiation ceremonies in other cultures have disappeared from ours. Our task is to invest our daughters' everyday care with purpose, intention, and awareness of their feminine value, and then to create celebrations to mark the passages in their lives. Broadly speaking, I use the word *celebration* to mean a conscious attention to making the girls in your life feel that they *matter*—to you, to the family, to the community, to the world.

An Overview

Celebrating Girls explores stories and celebrations for mothers, grandmothers, godmothers, and other women in intimate relationships with girls to daily support their femininity and celebrate meaningful passages in their lives. Each chapter addresses girls' development from birth to puberty. (A girl may have her first period as early as age nine or as late as age sixteen.) Many of the child-raising principles in this book also apply to boys, but here the focus is on girls. Each chapter highlights a positive aspect of intimate relationship with girls that has significance for feminine identity and self-esteem.

The theme of each chapter correlates with an aspect of a girl's development. For example, the theme of chapter 3 is "Bathing," and this chapter discusses water as a feminine element, the waters of the womb, and bathing as a purifying, renewing ritual. Water is associated with emotions, so chapter 3 also deals with emotional integrity in girls and suggests ways in which you can help nourish a deep, honest emotional life in your daughter. The themes of chapter 4, "Holding," chapter 9, "Strengthening Her Body," and chapter 10, "Walking into Beauty," which honor her body's uniqueness and encourage sports and a healthy relationship to menstruation, are linked with assuring her physical self-confidence and developing a positive body image. Chapter 5, "Haircombing," discusses the everyday ritual of combing and doing her hair. Symbolically, hair is related to a woman's thoughts, so this chapter deals with empowering a girl's mind. Chapter 6, "Dressing," talks about clothing and relates it to her social development with peers, family, and community. Chapter 7, "Adorning," takes up the ancient symbolism of jewelry as feminine value as well as girls' fascination with cosmetics and their containers. It discusses a girl's involvement in the arts—drama, music, singing, painting—as another avenue for self-expression. This chapter also addresses making meaning of life and touches on a girl's spiritual development. In chapter 8, "Storytelling," telling stories and reading to your daughter are presented as valuable for both bonding with her and for teaching her about feminine history.

In every chapter, I have included some significant motifs from girls' rites of passage ceremonies around the world that honor a girl's femininity and enhance her sense of self-worth, while eliminating those which serve to repress or degrade girls and women. These motifs are simply points of departure to help you nurture and empower your daughters. Use your imagination and what you know about your own daughter, granddaughter, niece, or "little sister" to create your own celebrations for her. If you are a girl reading this book, you may have creative ideas to suggest to your mother. At the back of the book, in addition to the bibliography, is a resource guide that lists reference books and organizations that are working to promote self-esteem and health for girls (and women) in our society.

I have also taken into account that most traditional tribal ceremonies assume a girl is marriageable and ready for childbirth once her first menstruation ceremony is accomplished. In those cultures, a woman's identity will revolve around being a mother, wife, and homemaker. In our culture, the pivotal moment of first menstruation marks and ushers in a period of adolescence. The multiple identities that a woman lives today require a delicate balancing, not only between her feminine and masculine sides, but also between her inner and outer worlds. Therefore, I have tried to answer the question of what kind of upbringing would best suit the emerging feminine identity of a menstruating adolescent that includes her inner moon cycle, her developing sexuality, and her probable progression toward being a woman functioning in the world of work outside the home.

At the end of *Reviving Ophelia*, Mary Pipher seems to share the collective intuition of women I know when she says, "As a culture, we could use more wholesome rituals for coming of age. Too many of our current rituals involve sex, drugs, alcohol, and rebellion. We need more positive ways to acknowledge growth, more ceremonies and graduations. It's good to have toasts, celebrations and markers for teens that tell them, 'You are growing up and we're proud of you.'"

Shepherding girls through the difficult preteen to teenage time requires a firm and loving attitude on the part of parents. We have to monitor their world closely, but we also have to accept that their world is very challenging. It is good if we begin celebrations before our daughters become teenagers and start to slip away into their peer culture. This will give us a strong foundation for a relationship with them, and they will already know how to make wise choices.

Having been praised as young girls, with our faith in them demonstrated, they will move into preteen and adolescent waters with a solid base for increasing independence, social responsibility, and self-confidence. They will feel empowered by their mothers, who let them test their capabilities, and then celebrate them at every stage of their development. They will be strong enough to choose healthy rites of passage over unhealthy ones. And they will be centered enough to feel the stirrings of their sexuality and to get to know those desires without falling into desperate attachments to boys, or feeling themselves worthless without a boy's attention.

This book is dedicated to showing how we can bring our feminine wisdom to bear on giving every girl in our lives a multitude of reasons to celebrate who she is.

TWO

■ ■ ■

Raising a Daughter

M Y ELEVEN-YEAR-OLD DAUGHTER, Lia, and I are sitting at the kitchen counter drinking tea. As she adds spoonfuls of sugar to her cup, she is recounting to me the play of the day's events in her sixth-grade class. She tells me what happened between her girlfriends, "the boys," and her teachers. She shares her personal joys and difficulties: her relay race time (only one second off from the highest fitness award), her A on an Egyptian project (a total preoccupation for the past month), her newly beaded necklace breaking and spilling all over the classroom floor (spoiling several hours of concentrated work). I respond in quick succession with praise, delight, and sympathy. We giggle together at a teacher's rude remark, overheard by chance in the corridor, and exchange knowing glances over a boy's disruptive antics in Spanish class. Sometimes I am reminded of a similar experience of my own when I was her age and tell her that story. She, in turn, asks about my day, and I recount my small satisfactions and frustrations about home, work, or writing. This is the fabric of our mother-daughter relationship, a weaving back and forth out of which our mutual understanding is daily renewed.

One fall day, when Lia asked, "How was your day, Mom?" I told her my idea for this book. A friend and I had had a long discussion about a question that women often ask me when I lecture on girls' rites of passage in other cultures: "Where are the modern ceremonies with which to raise my daughter, celebrate her femininity, enhance her self-esteem, and help her with all the transitions from infancy to girlhood and adolescence?" I told Lia that I wanted to write a book celebrating girls, for all women—mothers, friends, aunts, grandmothers—who wish to have close relationships with the next generation of girls in their lives. Lia perked up and said excitedly, "Oh, do write about it, Mom! I'll help. Can I be in it? I want to choose a name for the book."

I felt my own creativity stirred by Lia's enthusiastic response and began to think about all the conversations I have with women friends, clients, and colleagues, voicing our concerns about our daughters. In the midst of our busy lives, it often seems difficult for us to mother our daughters in a deep way. We organize our households, see that our families are clothed and fed, and try to keep up with our children's over-full schedules, as well as our own. But mothering a daughter in order to nurture and empower her femininity seems to elude many of us. I thought about distressed adolescent girls in therapy, who often burst into tears when asked, "Who are you as a woman?" They have no idea what it means to be a woman or to be feminine. No one has taught them about their feminine history, their female bodies, their female minds, or their feminine souls.

As I began to write, *Celebrating Girls* became a wonderful mother-daughter collaboration. Lia read each chapter as it was written and gave me valuable responses, questioning words and phrases that were unclear to her and offering suggestions from her own life. As the book developed, friends of ours contributed their own experiences of being mothers, stepmothers, daughters, aunts, cousins, or teachers to girl children. Child therapists offered stories from their work with girls. And Lia polled her friends for their favorite ways of being celebrated by the women in their lives. The result is the book you are holding in your hands—a book designed to help you nurture and empower the girls in your life.

Empowering the Mother-Daughter Relationship

I strongly believe that the mother-daughter relationship is the ground for teaching, talking, and sharing the feminine experience and that the more we empower that experience, the healthier our girls will be. We need to secure our daughters' sense of self-worth, in their minds and their bodies, so that they will not turn away from us and from themselves. When male authority dominates, girls lose touch with central parts of themselves and with their mothers in attempts to identify with men. That is why girls radically shift their attention to boys at adolescence, influenced by school socialization and being treated in increasingly trivialized or denigrating ways as they approach puberty. They become the objects of boys' lives instead of being the subjects of their own lives.

Putting the male at the center often continues long past puberty. Many women I have seen in psychotherapy who realize that they have always felt they were "nothing without a man" have said to me: "I rejected my mother and in so doing, I rejected myself." But when the mother-daughter bond is a strong, supportive one, a young girl can feel proud of being female and validated in her femininity.

With attention, interest, and empathy for your daughter, you can use your feminine power to empower her. Your relationship will foster her growth emotionally, psychologically, and intellectually, and, in turn, nurture you too. You will both feel more joyous, healthy, energized, and free. You will learn from each other. When a girl's mother is absent, this role can be taken on by a grandmother, aunt, or a close female friend of the family. But a girl does need a primary girl-to-woman relationship in her life: to be able to see and hear women talk about femininity and what it means to be a woman. If her mother or other trusted woman has modeled femininity in her life, a girl will see herself mirrored. She has someone to emulate. Her father or other men cannot mirror her femininity in this way. Female role models are the most important factor in her developing a high sense of self-efficacy, that is, her belief that she is competent to succeed at a particular task.

If you are the mother of a daughter, encourage her also to have close relationships with grandmothers, godmothers, and your friends, who may each have something different to offer her as she matures. A girl may be drawn to a particular woman, for example, a teacher, therapist, stepmother, or special friend, who can also guide her with informal long talks and celebrations of femininity. Such a mentor can also fill in for an absent mother. Single-parent fathers should help facilitate the presence of such mentors in their daughters' lives.

What Happens in Her Body Happens in Her Mind

Such empowerment is crucial for girls, because our essential female biology forms the base of a different psychological, emotional, and social identity that is quite different from men. Each one of us has an individual mix of so-called masculine and feminine traits in body chemistry as well as in behavior. Modern women have learned to work and compete with men on men's terms and have very developed masculine sides. But now it is time for women to reclaim themselves, their feminine identities, their feminine intuition, and to teach their daughters to honor their femininity. Girls' differences from boys need to be acknowledged so our daughters will be strong in who they are.

We need to teach our daughters that what happens in their bodies also happens in their minds. From the beginning of history, cultures have created ceremonies to mark our passage from one stage of life to another; ceremony serves an emotional and developmental need for the individual, a cultural need for the group. Each transition in a girl's or woman's life—from puberty to menopause—is a dramatic physical event that affects her mind and soul. It makes sense then, that each step of healthy feminine development or change calls for a response that acknowledges its meaning. Ceremonies define meaning, and celebrating a girl's femininity enhances her self-esteem.

To feel whole and to live from a place of wholeness in herself, a girl needs to be in touch with her femininity. This is a subtle yet critical process that ceremonies help reinforce. Then her feminine consciousness will function in the world in a grounded, centered, and productive way. This includes an understanding of our female bodies and our cycles, an understanding of women as potential vessels of life, and of female psychology mirroring our bodies' potential.

Such inner awareness may be at odds with a girl's peers' attitudes toward their bodies and feelings. But if the adult women in a girl's life gently persist in supporting her life-giving femininity, she is able to mature with deep strength.

Yearnings for modern feminine ceremonial celebrations are particularly strong in women whose daughters are approaching their first menstruation. As a girl approaches this important change, the whole experience of the mother-daughter bond from birth to puberty comes to the fore. When her body begins to change and she has her first period, a girl raised on feminine ground will be empowered to find her adolescent identity with grace and assurance. Although it is best to foster this consciousness from birth, it will have great value whenever you begin. It is never too late to amplify the value of the feminine for your daughter. We can begin to celebrate our daughters and give them meaningful initiations at any age.

Intimate Time Is Sacred Time

Raising girls in a celebratory way that honors the sacred quality of the feminine requires intimacy with the girl in your life. Our society is so rushed, so achievement oriented and materialistically driven, that we often have not been taught how to create quiet time, downtime, for ourselves or for our girls. The popularity of recent books, such as Sue Bender's *Everyday Sacred*, that emphasize finding the soul in everyday life shows how hungry our culture is for a greater dimension of meaning in the busyness of the world. The ground for celebrating girls is to teach them to appreciate quiet time alone, to listen to their own feelings, thoughts, and dreams. Self-esteem is built on the foundation of strong inner lives; a girl with a strong sense of who she is and what she believes in will not succumb to destructive peer pressure. You too will have to make time for this kind of teaching. Girls need cyclical solitude or introversion for emotional and mental well-being. And when they begin to menstruate, their bodies will require a monthly attitude of retreat.

With good mothering, a girl begins at birth to form a positive feminine identity that culminates with her first period. Physically, psychologically, and emotionally, she will experience her womb preparing itself for conception, then cleansing itself each month. Most women feel a pull to turn inward either premenstrually or while they are bleeding. We can teach our young daughters to value turning inward at all stages of their lives, to appreciate the waxing and waning of a woman's psychological and physical energy.

Women and their daughters also need to have one-to-one time, preferably daily, when we can reinforce what girls feel and think, help them understand themselves, and teach them how to become empowered in a world still dominated by men. Appreciating time alone and intimate time together, we can begin to identify and mark our daughters' development with acts that help acknowledge the moment in some enduring way. This defines a girl to herself and to those around her and allows her to move on to the next stage or challenge with new energy and self-confidence.

Feminine Ceremonies

Instilling girls' lives with an awareness of their feminine gifts can take place in many ways, some large, some small. Having tea with my daughter to share the events of the day is a small everyday ritual. Chatting at bedtime while I comb her hair is another private time together with nurturing attention while I listen to her ideas. Less frequently, perhaps at the end of a busy week or after a long hike, Lia and I take a relaxing candlelit bath together.

If you begin to think about these ordinary moments with the girls in your life as meaningful, you will soon experience a shift in awareness that allows you to hold these times in a more sacred way. You will begin to know that a private talk or cuddle with your six year old at bedtime or your dialogue with your thirteen-year-old niece about getting a second pierce in her ear are valuable times that have implications far beyond the immediate feelings of either pleasure or duty. Such moments become a sacred ritual of valuing this girl for who she is.

We unofficially mark important transitions in girls' lives all the time. In the process of weaning from the bottle or the pacifier or tapering off with nursing, we may talk to her about being a big girl now. We may offer her a gift or a coveted toy when she has made the sacrifice of her earlier form of self-comfort. The gift symbolizes the rewards of taking the next step in growing up. For example, a friend of mine took her five-year-old daughter, who was having difficulty with the idea of leaving preschool, to the toy store on the morning of the first day of kindergarten as an incentive for the child to participate in this necessary step in her growth. Her daughter willingly participated from that time on. In many homes, when a child loses a tooth, she puts it under her pillow. The tooth fairy comes in the night, takes the tooth, and leaves a few coins in its place. This childhood custom marks a change, encourages discussion in the family about the child growing up, and acknowledges the loss of childhood.

Birthday parties are yearly rituals that take time out from everyday life to mark the years as we grow older. But the deeper meaning is to celebrate birth—the gift of life itself. As they mature, girls will be able to nurture life in their wombs. Many mothers find themselves mentally reliving their birth experiences on their children's birthdays. On each birthday, a girl gets to experience herself as special on her day. As we grow older, marking our birthdays also encourages us to assess where we are in our individual development. We evaluate the past year, try to make sense of it, and designate meaning to our experience as we engage in these annual celebrations.

You can celebrate girls by creating interesting ceremonies for them at important times: beginning preschool, grammar school, or middle school, performances, athletic games, or a job well done. You may honor girls' passages from one stage of life to another in either private or public ways. Emotionally, a celebration is a way of relieving anxiety, of resolving self-doubt or fear that is always present at transitional times. Whether she is going from preschool to kindergarten, from girlhood to adolescence, or facing her first cross-country meet, she needs ways to cope with the new challenge. Celebrations also enlarge the significance of a girl's life, which, internally, prepares her for her cycle of menstruation that begins with puberty.

In addition to these individual forms of celebrating our daughters, nieces, goddaughters, and "little sisters," it is also possible to infuse your family traditions and religious rituals with feminine values and with a sense of the sacred for your girls. At a family reunion, you can remember a special grandmother or great aunt with a toast or by reading a poem in her honor. When you trim a Christmas tree or light the Chanukah candles, you can draw attention to the role of the Madonna in Catholicism or to the Shekinah, the feminine aspect of God, in Judaism.

The possibilities for reinforcing and reflecting the value of the feminine for your daughters are endless. You will find it a continuous process of discovery. Through all of these forms, we are educating our daughters about what it means to be female in our culture.

Living the Myth of Demeter and Kore

As I watch Lia and her friends move toward coming of age, I am acutely aware of the need to celebrate, honor, and strengthen their femininity. I feel both excited about Lia's developing body and mind and sad at the loss of my little girl. I remember feeling this mixture of sadness and happiness at other turning points in her life. I felt it when she was almost five years old, on the verge of starting kindergarten, and decided to mark it for her and for myself with a special fifth-birthday party. Because her birthday falls in May, I decorated a maypole, using an old apricot tree in the front yard as the pole. As I tied multicolored ribbons on the tree, I thought about the move my daughter was about to make out of my protecting arms and into a larger world. At the party, she and her girlfriends danced around the tree, laughing and singing as they haphazardly wove the ribbons tight. While they danced, I silently wove my wishes for my daughter and her friends to make this passage securely and to embark on their grammar-school adventure with zest and confidence.

Six years later, on Mother's Day in May, Lia and I helped lead a mother-daughter ceremony and celebration at Green Gulch Farm, an American Zen Buddhist community in Muir Beach, California. Lia and I, together with a Zen priest and her prepubescent daughter, joined with other women from the community. We prepared a beautiful maypole and learned music, lyrics, and a weaving dance to teach to the group of eighty mothers and daughters who attended this event. The four of us, two mothers, two daughters, read and enacted the Greek myth of Demeter and Persephone, in which a daughter is separated from her mother, then reunited with her:

Kore, the daughter of Demeter, is picking flowers in a meadow with her girlfriends. As she reaches to pick a fragrant narcissus, the earth opens and Hades, king of the underworld, snatches her and takes her below in his golden chariot while she weeps and wails. Demeter, goddess of the earth, is so bereft at the loss of her daughter that she refuses to let anything grow. All the crops that sustain life on earth shrivel up, killing men and animals alike, until Zeus gives in and persuades Hades, his brother, to return Kore to her mother. Before she leaves the underworld, Kore eats some pomegranate seeds, which ensures that she will spend part of every year with Hades in the underworld. She becomes Persephone, Queen of Shades. When Persephone and her mother are reunited, they are both overjoyed. Demeter makes the ground fertile again and bestows gifts on the Greek people—the gift of grain and the gift of mysteries.

Psychologically, the story celebrates the emotional renewal that occurs in intimacy between mothers and daughters and the need for a girl to know both sides of her nature. Every year, Persephone returns to her mother in the Spring, then goes back to the underworld to join her husband, Hades, at the Fall Equinox. Demeter's gifts to the Greek people when she is reunited with her daughter are both physically and spiritually nourishing. When we celebrate our daughters, help their femininity flower, we bring Persephone back from the underworld and reestablish the balance between masculine and feminine in our lives.

Our enactment of the story at Green Gulch was brought poignantly to life by our daughters' being poised at the edge of adolescence. The maypole weaving on Mother's Day was more artistic and orderly than it had been at Lia's fifth-birthday party. But I know that her earlier experience of the maypole was reenacted in her wholehearted participation in a more elaborate version of that ceremony as a preteen girl.

The Mother-Daughter Mystery

For you, as a mother or aunt, ritualizing passages for your daughter is an opportunity to renew yourself. To celebrate your daughter is to celebrate yourself—this is the mother-daughter mystery. When Lia and I talk about her approaching first menstruation, I hear her mixed feelings and thoughts. She is losing her carefree childhood as she prepares to take up the responsibilities of a menstruating adolescent. Simultaneously, I am ambivalent about approaching menopause. I am losing my fertility as I prepare for life after childbearing. I also feel Lia separating from me and growing up. The mirror of that truth in me is that as she moves away, I lose my daughter yet I regain myself. I return to my individual life, changed and tempered by the intense experience of mothering young children. Her rite of passage at puberty will also internally mark that shift for me.

Such mother-daughter conversation comforts a girl in the midst of her emotional turmoil at puberty. One of Lia's favorite "coming of age" celebrations is the Navajo girl's puberty ceremony, the Kinaaldá; the girl is said to be "walking into beauty" throughout her four-day ritual. Lia loves drama and can relate to the Navajo tradition of adorning the girl with clothes, jewelry, and song. She does gymnastics and appreciates that the Navajo girl runs races and has a massage during her ceremony. Because Lia likes to spend time with me in the kitchen, the elaborate cake that the Navajo girl bakes—with the help of her mother and other women—also appeals to her. As we talk about these and other possibilities, Lia and I play with changing scenarios of how her rite of passage might be.

If you were not celebrated as a girl, did not have such ceremonies in your childhood, you can be replenished and nurtured through your daughter's or granddaughter's experience. Instead of passing on the cultural devaluation of the feminine to your own child, you can re-create your daughter and yourself and begin to respect your mature feminine cycles in a richer way. You may find your own self-confidence rising and that you are capable of being more effective at work and in your relationships.

Trust your instincts when celebrating the girls in your life. Depending on your girl's age, the passage being celebrated, and her temperament, you may create a ceremony for her that lasts for several days or one that takes place in ten minutes. Remember, creating time in the day for intimate or sacred moments is best. Marking the transition from one stage of life to another in a simple, spontaneous way is more important than letting it go by unnoticed, so seize the moment!

THREE

■ ■ ■

Bathing: Nourishing Emotional Integrity

I LOVED MOTHERING MY SON, my firstborn, but when my daughter was born I found myself delving into the mystery of her likeness to me, knowing that one day she too would bear life, if she chose. I remembered feelings that I had known with my mother, her grandmother; I saw my mother's face in Lia's face and rejoiced in her birth as my mother had in mine. In my Italian Catholic mother-daughter line, the female connection through the Virgin Mary back to the prehistoric Mother Goddess is powerfully alive. Giving birth to a girl revitalized that matriarchal tradition for me and deepened my relationship to the feminine spirit. In the early months of Lia's life, as I rocked and nursed her in the middle of the night, I watched the moon rise above a flowering apple tree through the window in her room. In the dark silence, as my milk flowed to nourish her, I was in turn nourished by my ancient moon mother.

Self-esteem for a girl begins at birth. Her first sense of self is a body sense. She has spent nine months developing in the safe, warm, nourishing waters of her mother's womb. All her one-to-one relationships with women will call up that original uterine existence. These are deep, intense, primordial feelings— "the knowledge flowing between two alike bodies," as the poet Adrienne Rich says. Mother-daughter, sister-sister, grandmother-granddaughter kinships reach backward and forward in an unbroken line of generational connectedness. Scientists have even discovered a component of mitochondrial DNA that has been passed down unchanged from mother to daughter from the beginning of human existence. Thus it is present in all women.

The essential body and mind relationship between mother and daughter is the unconscious ground of feminine psychology and of our lives as modern women and girls. Relationships between girls and women have this quality of shared nature. We are capable of basking in the bath of the feminine together, of coming together, of merging, then separating again. Girls and women who live together often menstruate at the same time of the month; their menstrual biological clocks synchronize.

In the waters of the womb, a girl experiences her first element of nature. Nature is important in feminine identity. Women's menstrual cycles reflect the cyclical nature of the earth, often following the changes in the moon, and are biologically related to the change of the seasons. Women's bodies respond with a decrease in the hormone melatonin in March near the Spring Equinox, and with an increase in this hormone in the Fall at the onset of Winter near the Fall Equinox. Their innate circadian clocks react first to the return of Spring, resetting themselves to keep pace with the extra daytime hours, then again resetting to synchronize with the darkness. By contrast, men's bodies do not respond to the change of the seasons, nor do they have a monthly cyclical rhythm.

If you have an infant daughter, try to expose her to natural settings—parks, beaches, woods. Whether you nurse her or bottle-feed her, she will take in the wind, the sun, and the sound of trickling creeks or ocean waves with her milk. And you too will be soothed and fed by the natural forces around you. The same is true as she grows older—try to be out in nature, near water together as much as possible. In the Chinese Book of Changes, the I Ching, water is the feminine element. In dreams, the ocean is the mother of all things.

Water is an element that traditionally has been associated with psychic powers and meditation. In Marion Zimmer Bradley's book, *The Mists of Avalon*, Morgaine, the high priestess of Avalon, seeks her visions on a mountain at a place where the stream forms a natural rock pool. There she meditates, looking into the water, seeing at first her own face reflected, then, gradually, scenes that show her role in the political-social-religious context of King Arthur's court. The psychological meaning of this use of water is self-reflection. If you create time in your girls' lives for self-reflection, they will be able to access their inner selves. Questions will bubble up in them about what they observe in their lives. They will find ways to nurture themselves, to resolve inner conflicts, and to decide where they want to put their energy in their lives. They will know when they need to ask for help. Teaching your daughter to treasure time to herself is one of the greatest gifts that you can give her.

Self-reflection is also crucial for you. Your welcoming of your daughter at birth and your welcoming of girls into your life will both depend on and influence your own sense of feminine self-esteem. Think about your adult relationship to the "feminine bath." Do you occasionally immerse yourself in the company of other women with whom you can share deep feelings about being female, both positive and negative, and feel heard, understood, and appreciated? Do you need more introversion in your life? The early months of your daughter's life, while nursing or feeding her, is a perfect time to let yourself indulge in self-reflection. Whatever your girl's age, find a little time to yourself to turn inward.

Self-nurturing for a woman requires an attitude of feminine-valuing. It is enhanced by time in which you shift your attention to yourself, either alone or with other women. Whether you are a high-powered lawyer working in a big city or a dairy farmer in the Midwest, you need to nurture yourself. If you do, the choices you make in your life will be conscious and empowered.

Do you take time out for your menstrual periods or turn your attention inward during that time? Do you take other time for yourself, self-renewing time, away from the hubbub of your family, job, volunteer work, or social life? What do you find nurturing: a walk in the woods or a drive to the beach; having your nails done or your hair colored; writing down your dreams at sunrise or taking a hot bath at bedtime; having lunch with a close woman friend or going away on a weekend retreat? Self-nurturing feminine time for yourself helps you nurture the girls in your life. By example, you show them the value of self-renewal.

Renewal in the Feminine Waters

Water is also a purifying element. In ancient Greece, temples of healing were always located near bodies of water. The waters of springs, lakes, and rivers were thought to have powers to heal the mind, the soul, and the body. Greek Hygeia, the first known woman physician, to whom we owe our English word *hygiene*, was the first to recognize the value of cleanliness for healing the sick. The Greek goddesses Aphrodite and Hera returned to their temple homes once a year for a sacred bath in the holy spring that was said to renew their virginity.

Water is renewal, re-sacralization. In psychotherapy, as women learn to nurture and value their feminine ways of thinking and feeling, their dreams are often full of watery images: spraying fountains, overflowing bathtubs, indoor pools, bottomless lakes. In the unconscious, the feminine waters are rising in these women, rising to dissolve rigid patterns of thought and feeling, often based in their fathers' way of thinking, as feminine nature seeks expression.

In Catholicism, the first sacrament is Baptism. In this ceremony, a newborn child is blessed with holy water to symbolize birth into a spiritual life. Originally, Baptism required a complete immersion of the child in a stream or river. Now churches have holy-water fountains, and the priest pours or sprinkles water over the baby's head. This ceremony had a surprising impact on Adrienne when she baptized her first daughter. Adrienne had a difficult delivery with Anne; she hemorrhaged and had to spend several days in the hospital. When she returned home with Anne, she remembers being very weepy; her emotions swung dramatically from one extreme to the other. When Anne was three weeks old, Adrienne decided to have her baptized. Anne's father, although not a practicing Catholic himself, supported his wife's decision because he knew how much it meant to her to raise her daughter in this religious tradition.

At the baptismal ceremony, Adrienne's tears flowed from beginning to end. It was the first choice she was making for her daughter and her first step as a mother in relation to her community. It was an intimate family occasion. Adrienne's mother, father, and other close relatives were there; the priest who baptized Anne was Adrienne's cousin. "I was coming home to my own tradition," Adrienne said. The baptismal waters introduced Anne into the spiritual life of her family, while Adrienne's tears were an expression and affirmation of her power as a wife and mother. The decision had taken assertion on her part; her tears were a sign of her strength.

Some cultures have public baths where women go to bathe and talk and groom themselves. The ancient Romans had pools for exercise along with steam rooms. Our modern gyms owe something to these ancient gymnasiums. The mikvah is a bath where Jewish women go to purify and renew themselves after their menstrual periods. They abstain from sexual relationship during their periods; this gives them time to turn inward, to pay attention to their own needs. When I was in graduate school, I swam every day in the outdoor pool, surrounded by neoclassical columns and marble benches, in the women's gymnasium. I relished leaving the bustling, colorful campus scene and walking through the swinging doors into the cool, dark women's locker room. After my refreshing swim under the open sky, I returned to shower and dress among women who were sharing the "feminine bath" together.

Honoring All Her Feelings

Water also symbolizes emotions. Our feelings ebb and flow, sometimes flooding us, but always changing. Raise your daughters with emotional integrity by helping them to be emotionally real to themselves and others. Honor all of her expressions of feeling. When she is a baby, this means understanding that she has to cry and fuss as she adjusts to this new world. When she is a toddler, it means knowing that her tantrums are a legitimate venting of her frustration—she is expressing herself in a healthy way. When she is a preteen and begins to withdraw from you or express anger toward you, it means understanding that she needs to separate from you as she begins to move toward adolescence.

With an infant or young child, it is best to hold her while she calms herself. When she is older, you can both honor her feelings and reassert the peace of your household by putting her in her room with a calm and empathic comment about her being upset and needing time alone to work it through. So long as she is not hurting herself or destroying her room, or does not feel abandoned, this validates her need to experience her distress. When she returns from an episode like this, give her a big hug and kiss and try to resume whatever you were doing with her. From the very beginning, she is learning from you a way of coping with distress and crisis.

Girls need to learn to own their whole experience, including the emotions and thoughts that are not generally socially acceptable. This goes against the prevailing cultural code of being "good" that is forced on girls. Being "good" means not making noise, not being aggressive, and not disturbing anyone. Yet your daughter's self-esteem is based on being able to accept all of her thoughts and feelings as valid and being able to express them in safe ways. One minute, she will say that she hates you or her father; the next minute, she will want a hug from one of you. One day after school, she'll tell you that she's never speaking to her best friend again; that evening, she will be planning an overnight with her. Vacillating, ambivalent feelings are part of growing up and developing emotional maturity. As a mother, it is easy to get caught up in the tide of your daughter's feelings and try to solve her problems for her. But it is best to ride the waves with her, maintaining some inner detachment so that you do not get invested in either extreme.

Although all feelings are acceptable, what she does with her feelings is another matter. Meredith always told her stepdaughter, Cheryl, that it was fine to feel any way she felt, but that that didn't mean she could hurt herself or another person, physically or emotionally, as a consequence of those feelings. In this way, she began to teach Cheryl to separate feeling from impulsive action. Causing physical pain to another is an easy boundary to define for your daughter, but emotional boundaries are more difficult to describe and monitor. It is good as a mother to have tolerance for preteen and teenage girls' impulsive, dramatic expressions of negative feelings. But you need to draw the line when either of you threaten to become emotionally abusive.

Her rage will hurt not only you but also her, and vice versa. Recent scientific research has discovered negative psychological effects of anger on the expressor as well as on the recipient of an angry outburst. If someone is in a rage, her heartbeat escalates, her muscles tense, and she may have trouble breathing. Furthermore, the more irritable, tense, and angry she becomes, the more predisposed to angry outbursts she becomes, because the structures and chemicals in the brain that control strong feelings become habituated to triggering impulsive anger. Therefore, it's important to try to handle your daughter's and your own anger in constructive ways to keep the communication between you open. When arguments are heating up, take time out for each of you to cool down—research shows that it takes twenty minutes for the rush of chemicals to subside. Do your best to maintain your feelings of love for her in the face of anger. Express that love when the storm abates and anytime you find an appropriate opening for it.

In emotionally neutral moments, help your daughter accept, move through, and resolve her feelings and plan action. If she is acting out her feelings in inappropriate ways at school or at home, talk to her about the feelings and help her figure out healthier ways to express them. But do not label the feelings "bad."

In middle school, girls often have a lot of up and down angry feelings with their friends. Theresa's family of four spends most of their free time together. But when her twelve-year-old daughter, Tabitha, is having a problem, she seeks her mother out to talk, without her younger brother or father in the picture. Recently, Tabitha confided in her mother that she was furious at her longtime girlfriend, who was suddenly refusing to sit or play with her at lunch period. Theresa told me, "I remember being her age. It comes to me so clearly when she talks, how it made me so mad. I just got an attitude about people who hurt me, but I want Tabitha to be able to deal with her problems differently. I also want her to have compassion." Theresa encouraged Tabitha to give her friend the benefit of the doubt and to talk to her about the rejection. Tabitha did, heard it as her friend's problem, and sought out other girls to be with at recess. After a few months, her friend started approaching her again. Theresa said, "No one ever talked to me about life and how to handle situations when I was a child. I learned everything the hard way—from experience. I love being close with Tabitha."

Anger is not the only shadowy emotion that girls may feel. Feelings of sadness, shame, loss, anxiety, or fear (to mention only a few) are also part of girls' experience. Girls lose confidence as they disown themselves, as they replace their own experience with others' view of their experience. When your daughter says she feels happy, it is probably easier to mirror her feelings for her and share her joy. But when she says she feels bad or that something is wrong, it is often more difficult for mothers.

Girls whose temperament predisposes them to act everything out can be particularly trying. Try to pay special attention, take time out, sit with her, to find out the feelings beneath her actions. Listen, sympathize, see it from her point of view. Above all, believe her. Use your own discriminating judgment as you listen.

Whether it is her woman dance teacher or her male English teacher, if your daughter feels something is amiss with an interaction, try to listen from your own feminine core to get a sense of what the teacher is missing. Do not assume that the adult in her scenario is right; often the adult is wrong. When a problem persists, arrange a conference with the three of you, where both of them can air their grievances and you can hopefully help facilitate a resolution. Having a conference with the teacher models for your daughter a healthy way to resolve a problem. The three of you may come to a new understanding that allows your daughter and the teacher to grow in their work together, or you may find there is an irreconcilable impasse.

If you hear that the teacher has a legitimate concern, voice your support of the teacher in the meeting and help your daughter think of ways to change her behavior. If you see that the teacher is being unfair, voice your concern about your daughter's feelings to the teacher. After the meeting, problem-solve with your daughter about how to handle the situation. If it is a ballet class, she may be able to change teachers by changing her lesson time, day, or studio. But if it is her grammar-school teacher, she is probably stuck with the same teacher all year. In that case, it's important to discuss coping skills with her. How can she get along in class, knowing she and the teacher have differences? And how can she manage to get the most out of her studies in spite of it?

Airing feelings often brings a strong sense of emotional well-being and resolution. Your confidence and faith will give her confidence in herself. Such a process empowers her; it keeps her from feeling like a passive victim, because she has a way to handle the situation. Such coping skills will be helpful to her later in life when she has to work with other incompatible people.

Sharing Painful Feelings

Listening to the girls in your life and hearing the range of their emotions will bring up your own feelings, some of which are painful. Crying with your daughter or granddaughter over some disturbing event, whether the death of a pet, a confrontation with evil in a book she is reading, or a shameful feeling that she has about something that happened at school, can be healing for both of you. Give her and yourself permission to cry to express feelings. Mothers often find themselves trying to edit feelings in their children that are difficult for them. They particularly tend to react negatively to characteristics in their daughters that they dislike in themselves. For example, Rita's mother hated the way she looked. Because Rita looked very much like her, her mother continually tried to revise Rita's appearance by suggesting that her daughter bleach her hair and have cosmetic surgery on her eyes and ears. Rita valiantly resisted her mother's impositions: "My reaction was 'No way! I'm not doing it!' I learned very young that she was projecting her self-hatred on me and that I had to separate myself from her." Rita was strong enough to maintain her sense of self but sadly missed the feminine nurturing that a mother can provide.

Rita's mother is an extreme example of the difficult feelings that daughters can bring up. But many women and girls express sorrow at having been rejected by their mothers in inexplicable ways. To be available to your daughter, *as she truly is*, it is essential to give some thought to your own experience as a girl, to what influenced you and contributed to the adult woman you are now. Were you encouraged to speak your mind, name your feelings, and stand up for your core knowing? Who responded to your needs as an infant? Who listened to your voice as a little girl, a maiden, a teenager? Were all your feelings honored? Did your mother set an example for self-nurturing? What were the guidelines for how you ate, how you expressed yourself? What kinds of behaviors were named feminine or masculine?

If your mother was not available to you as a child, did you have a special aunt or godmother or a friend's mother who paid particular attention to you? As you think about these questions, trust your thoughts and feelings as they come up in the moment. Your intuition and memory through such self-reflection is feminine knowledge. Let your mind-body knowing come to the fore and become the bedrock of how you relate to your daughter or granddaughter. She will be validated and so will you; you will both be empowered.

Women who have had difficult relationships with their own mothers are often fearful of having a daughter. Perhaps your mother was not able to share herself, to be in the "feminine bath" with you. Perhaps she did not listen to and accept the ebb and flow of your emotions and help you stay connected to your own watery essence. Perhaps she was out of touch with or afraid of her own feminine depths. But even if you did not have a positive relationship with your mother, you can renew yourself through caring for your own daughter. Those feminine depths are in you and you can realize them, access them as an adult, through self-reflection and contact with young girls, who have not yet been silenced by adults and society.

Bringing On the Waters

Use the element of water. Get back in touch with yourself by taking a leisurely warm bath or a stimulating shower, gazing into a lake, or walking by a stream. Explore ways to use nature to restore your vitality on a more regular basis. Find women friends with whom to share creative ways of affirming yourselves as women. A long hike in the woods on the weekend can be restorative. Sort your priorities and sift your choices to learn what is good for you on a given day.

Seek the companionship of women whose feminine values you share and respect. Several women I know make a periodic weekend retreat to a hot springs together, where they enjoy warm mineral soaks and mud baths. They renew their relationships to one another and to themselves through these ritual immersions in the "feminine bath." Enclosed in a private room where their bodies are being nurtured, they make this a time when they can all say what they feel and think, without censorship. This is sacred time, away from the ordinary. These women experience a tremendous revitalization of energy when they return from their retreat.

If you did not have a good relationship with your mother as a foundation for your femininity, it will be all the more challenging if your daughter has a temperament that threatens your sense of self-worth. But it is still possible to give her a positive experience of being female, even if you have a difficult relationship with her. Choose a water activity that she loves to minimize the chance of friction arising. Or plan a trip to a waterslide park. Try to understand what aspects of daily life are difficult for your daughter and plan positive time together that takes those difficulties into account. For example, if she has trouble with transitions, give her a lot of lead time to get ready for the event. If she gets hungry frequently, take along small snacks and drinks in the car. Instead of trying to accomplish a task or run errands, try to maximize the fun in your time out together. You will feel much better about yourself as a mother if the two of you have a good time. Whether you fish, sail, water-ski, or swim, you can explore feminine sharing in relation to water, even with a young girl. (And you never know when a girl may be inspired to become a marine biologist or an oceanographer.)

If your relationship to your daughter is a constant emotional struggle, ceremonies will provide a contained and rewarding way to honor the positive bond between you. Take a river trip with your older daughter, where the challenge, hard work, and exhilaration of rafting will crowd out her usual preteen preoccupations. You will both be relieved not to be butting heads over the same issues of whether she cleaned up her room, fed the cat or walked the dog, did her homework, or can go to a party without adult supervision.

Keeping our girls connected to their own watery depths, to their emotional depths, is valuable. From the time your daughter is born, you can make baths a ritual time for the two of you. You can create a quiet, peaceful time away from the busyness of the day. Put her infant bathtub under a musical mobile that plays a nursery song. Or take a bath with her and enjoy the warm water, like that of the womb, together. Elizabeth, now twelve years old, remembers her mother singing her to sleep. Jeannette, who writes the lyrics for her musician husband's songs, says that she sang to Elizabeth all the time, while nursing, bathing her, or soothing her when she was cranky. Gradually, singing Elizabeth to sleep became their nightly bedtime ritual.

If your baby girl does not find a warm bath soothing, you need to go more slowly with educating her to appreciate water. Pay attention to sudden transitions in temperature for her body. It is better to warm a room before you undress her; let her get used to the feel of the air on her bare skin, then slowly immerse her in warm water. Remember, she came from warm amniotic water to air abruptly, and she is still adjusting to this new element. Even breathing and the sensation of clothes touching her skin are new.

Preschool girls often enjoy taking a bath with a friend on an overnight. This is even more fun if you provide them with brightly colored bath crayons and water toys. Taking your daughter into the swimming pool with you can be a wonderful sharing experience if you are sensitive to her. When your daughter is learning to swim, you can use bath time to help reduce her fear of the water.

Stacey's daughter, Becky, walked off the edge of a swimming pool when she was two years old, sinking straight to the bottom. Stacey, an experienced swimmer, dived in and rescued her, but Becky developed a fear of putting her head underwater. When she was four years old, her parents gave her swimming lessons with a young man instructor who was very patient, played games with Becky, and never forced her to put her face in the water. Then at the last lesson, he took a chance and dunked her, thinking it would be all right. Becky was enraged and refused to have anything to do with him ever again. Stacey realized that she simply had to back off and wait until Becky was ready. So she told her daughter that next time it would be Becky's choice to take lessons. It took Becky two years to work through her fear and resume lessons. Stacey had to balance her own wish to make her daughter water-safe with her daughter's need for autonomy. And she chose to pay attention to her daughter's feelings.

From a young age, a girl can learn to use bathing as a time to center herself as well as to wash her body. A bath ritual is beneficial after any time that she has been very extroverted. When she has been camping out on a school field trip or involved in a strenuous sport activity, plan time when she returns for her to soak in a hot tub. A bubble bath is good for respecting her privacy when she begins to become modest about her body. Not only will the dirt dissolve, but she will have time to reflect on her time away. She may want to be alone or to share her thoughts and feelings with you. It will also help her return to herself, psychologically and emotionally, after days or nights of being with others.

If you help your daughter appreciate the emotional and psychological (as well as practical) uses of a bath, she will carry it with her into her womanhood as a positive resource for well-being. When she reaches high school and is feeling rejected by the girl who was her best friend in grammar school, or she is feeling humiliated and embarrassed by a boy's insensitive treatment of her, she will have a consoling ritual of self-renewal to turn to, rather than drugs or alcohol. There by candlelight, with her favorite music playing, she can soothe her feelings and think her own thoughts. Or she may find herself leaving the house to go sit by a pond or stream in an adjacent park to rebalance herself. The next day, she will be better prepared to face what comes at school, where peer relationships are all-important. Learning ways to calm herself, to restore herself, is critical for a girl's development.

Special baths are also wonderful before a party or occasion in a girl's life, where her bathing, dressing, and adorning prepare her for the experience emotionally as well as physically. Whether it is a spelling bee or a speech contest, her eighth-grade graduation dance, or the first day at a new school, candlelight and music, which both mark sacred time, help create a mood for a special bath. The first time your daughter wants to shave her legs and underarms could also be enhanced by a special bath.

Bathing does not have to be confined to bathrooms. You can take advantage of any body of water, manmade or natural. Swimming pools, hot tubs, or hot springs are great places for bath celebrations. Ponds, streams, and oceans also offer opportunities, spontaneous or planned. You can create a simple, memorable ritual while splashing in a mountain stream on a hot Summer day or wading in the pounding surf at the beach. These are also opportunities for telling stories of your own girlhood.

Tell your daughter or granddaughter about your own experience of the ocean, or streams, or learning to swim as a child. Or perhaps you lived in a desert or on plains and did not see bodies of water in nature. Whatever your experience, your daughter will benefit from knowing about it. Remember, you are talking about the ebb and flow of emotional life when you talk about water. It is easier to share your emotions with her, both present and past, with water around you. Some of what you share will wash away; some will stay and become part of the strong inner emotional sea that she is developing.

Girls start feeling moody in their prepubescent years, to experience ups and downs, and begin to turn inward. These feelings are similar to those that recur each month in their menstrual cycle; they become part of a shifting inner pattern in adulthood. Notice your own moods as you move through your monthly cycle; each woman is slightly different. If you recognize and acknowledge your own pattern, you can access your cycle as a self-renewing source and teach your daughter or the girls in your life to do the same. With this self-awareness on your part, you will celebrate with, not only for, the girls in your life.

Although the celebration may be for her, you will reap an inner reward—a deepening of your own emotions and a revitalization of your self-confidence as a woman.

FOUR

Holding:
Assuring Physical
Self-Confidence

ROSE WAS A MASSAGE THERAPIST when her infant daughter, Daria, was born. Often when her daughter was cranky or irritable or had trouble falling asleep, Rose would give her a light massage, using some lovely scented oil. Daria always fell asleep, relaxed and nurtured by her mother's touch. Rose enjoyed nursing Daria, but giving her massage was a different kind of nurturance. It was satisfying for Rose to be able to comfort her daughter in this unique way.

From the time your daughter is born, you hold her infant body. Your touch helps her develop—her first thoughts and feelings arise from your touch. Touch transforms; distressed infants are calmed by being picked up, cradled, and pacified by their mothers' hands. Touch is so vital that babies who are fed and clothed yet not held and cuddled fail to thrive. Touch fosters self-possession in a girl. That leads to psychological possession which means possessing her own life. Your daughter needs to be nursed and kissed, held and contained, for she learns to love and to love her own body through the love and respect that is shown her. Caressing voices, gentle handling, attention to her warmth or coolness, responding to her hunger—all are expressions of love and welcoming that validate her body and its needs.

Healthy intimacy, trust, and self-empowerment all begin with touch for a girl child, because empowerment lies in following the body, not in imposing control from outside. Touch also contributes to her sense of body affirmation, perception, and definition. A girl who has been touched in a loving and respectful way will instinctively reject any intrusion on her body. As you bathe and dress your daughter or assist her in doing it for herself, teach her to honor her body through the gentleness and firmness of your hands. In many families, these activities involve relationship and touch with brothers and sisters as well as mother or father. Healthy physical boundaries with others develop naturally in the course of these routine nurturing acts.

Self-exploration of her body should be respected. It is natural for little girls to touch their own bodies. Include her genitals when you teach your daughter the names of the parts of her body. When you see her touching herself, tell her, in age-appro-priate ways, that this behavior belongs to her private time alone. Nonjudgmental approval of this behavior will pave the way for her confiding in you about her developing body and eventually her sexual interest.

Body image becomes increasingly complex as a girl grows, and her body begins to change in preadolescence. At that time, her body image will be influenced by her peer culture's view of a desirable female body. The natural weight gain that she experiences as a preteen with hormonal activation may embarrass her. She will suddenly find herself part of our sexualized culture that views women as objects. She will compare herself to her friends and to the images she sees in magazines. But if her body and its needs have been affirmed, she will be able to stay grounded in her self-perception throughout puberty.

When she is an infant and preschooler, fostering her sense of empowerment means observing her body rhythms and fol-lowing them. Children vary widely in their innate sleep patterns. She may wake at six A.M. and take a three-hour nap in the after-noon, or sleep until eight or nine in the morning and not nap at all. Whatever her pattern, following her natural rhythms will ground her in her internal core from birth. As she grows older, continuing to honor her inner rhythm, as much as is possible within the family pattern, preschool, or daycare program, gives her the best opportunity to feel and respect her own individual physical needs.

Girls thrive on intimacy with you. Twelve-year-old Giovanna says that her most cherished time with her mother, Francesca, is when her mother sits on her bed, reads to her, and talks to her before she goes to sleep each night. When Giovanna was little, her mother used to get in bed with her while she read. When she turned off the light to snuggle with Giovanna until she fell asleep, sometimes Francesca would fall asleep first. Giovanna used to say, "I have a magic bed because it makes Mommy fall asleep, too." Now Giovanna feels possessive of her evening talks with her mother away from her younger sister, her father, and grand-mother. Try to make some time alone with each of your girls.

Eating is another area in which biological needs vary dra-matically for babies and children. You should give your daughter a healthy choice of foods and allow her to eat when she is hun-gry, and not use food to distract her from other needs. This is especially important for girls in our culture, where the societal value on women being thin has reached pathological propor-tions and eating disorders are rampant among teenage girls. It is catastrophic when food and eating revolve around control and power in a family. Instead, make food and eating nurturing activ-ities for yourself and your family. Never force a child to eat every-thing on her plate or withhold food from her as punishment. In psychotherapy, I see that women who battled with mothers who forced them to eat as toddlers or who used food to control their daughters in any way invariably have disturbed body images.

Mother-to-daughter education can provide a positive expe-rience of body knowledge that counteracts the cultural neurosis about women's bodies. When Vi delivered her son, her three teenage daughters frequently came to the hospital to visit her. When her milk came in, all three girls happened to be there. The nurse massaged Vi's breasts a little to relieve the pressure, and the milk squirted out and up to the ceiling. Emily, Vi's middle step-daughter, who had struggled all her life with a large-breasted, full figure, leaned over the bed while Vi was nursing. She said, "Do you think I'll ever be able to do that?" "Yes, of course!" Vi responded. Emily was worried that her breasts were too large for her to nurse!

Nurturing Positive Body Image

The way that you feel about your own body influences, to some degree, your daughter's feelings about hers. What image of your body did you have as you grew up? Would you have liked it to be different? If so, how can you help your daughter feel better about her body? Making it different for her may change how you feel about yours. If you feel grounded and confident as a woman in your body, you will naturally communicate that to your daughter.

If you feel insecure in your body, you may wish to find ways of honoring yourself with the power of touch. Find a masseuse; ask a friend or lover or mother to hold your hand, massage your shoulders, or give you some other physical (nonsexual) comfort. Begin to bless your own body, seeing it as a vessel of life, not as an object for others to desire or criticize. It is never too late for you to inhabit your body in a positive way.

With self-reflection, you can also offer your daughter posi-tive values around her female body. Small perceptions and actions count for a lot. You don't have to feel totally "realized" in every aspect of your life. Just appreciate the feel of her body in your arms for yourself and for her. Be glad that you can hold her when she is having an upset day. Be thankful that you can offer comfort and security; it will make all the difference in her life. If you begin to feel exhausted and frustrated, talk to sympathetic women friends about the difficulties of mothering a newborn. Or call your pediatrician's office and speak to the nurse, who can also refer you to a hot line or a counselor. There are many women in your community ready to help you as a mother keep perspective on the demands of your infant (or child of any age). And you may find feminine affirmation through your love for your daughter.

Paying Attention to Her Cues

Respect your daughter's individual body sense and privacy needs. Physical sensitivity varies from girl to girl. Doctor and dentist appointments can be made into events that help her develop her body boundaries. Teach appropriate regard for your daughter by telling doctors and nurses what you expect in terms of relationship to your child. When you take her to the pediatrician, if she does not want to take off her shirt and sit shivering in a thin paper gown, let her keep the shirt on until the doctor is ready. Then ask the doctor if he or she can use the stethoscope through her shirt. If the doctor cannot, you will still have shown your child that you considered her wishes and that she, too, can speak up about her feelings. If she is a child who is not bothered by the cooler temperature in the doctor's office, there is no need to bring up the issue. Pay attention to her cues.

Honor your daughter's right to monitor her physical boundaries. Perhaps the pediatric nurse's way is to tell her that the needle prick for a blood sample is not going to hurt. It's better to tell your child calmly that it will hurt a little, but that it will be over very quickly, and to help her focus on something else for the minute it takes to prick. Telling her the truth will reinforce the bond of trust between you and your girl. It will help her learn to trust her perception of pain and develop a tolerance for enduring minimal pain such as an injection when it is necessary for her health.

Consider the circumstances of the moment when planning an activity that involves your daughter's body. Remember that doctor's and dentist's examinations and treatments are intrusive procedures that she has to learn to submit to. Earn her cooperation by preparing her for them in an age-appropriate way. If, as a three year old, she has not had her nap, she is liable to be more resistant to a physical examination than if she were well rested. If, at five, she is having a tantrum in the waiting room at the dentist's office, consider that she may be feeling too vulnerable at this moment to have her teeth cleaned. Try to prepare her by talking to her about the visit in advance. If you know she is going to have a particularly grueling procedure, promise her an ice-cream cone or other treat after the visit. It will give her something to look forward to and be an incentive for her to endure discomfort. As she gets older, talk to her about your experiences with doctors and dentists and how you handle the discomfort that is sometimes involved. Talk to her too about your feelings of privacy with doctors who are new to you.

Changing Body Image at Adolescence

Body image is the main focus of the plunging self-esteem that so many girls experience in their preteen and adolescent years. Embarrassment about their bodies, fear of failure, depression at twice the rate of boys, and, by high school, high rates of unhappiness with themselves have all been noted by psychologist Carol Gilligan and many others. The problem lies in girls' attitudes toward their changing bodies. Therefore, one of the most important ways that you can help the girls in your life appreciate their bodies is by showing them that there are many different female body types and conveying the message that they are all beautiful.

Ruth, as a young single parent, used to take her daughter, Miriam, to Tassajara Hot Springs in Big Sur, California, for vacations. This Zen Buddhist monastery is built over hot sulfur springs deep in the mountains near Carmel. The natural water, renowned for its healing properties, is piped into separate bathhouses for men and women, next to a beautiful cold-water creek. There are showers and dressing rooms and one or two private baths for those wishing to be alone. A tranquil atmosphere prevails where the women and girls go to bathe. Ruth remembers how wonderful it was for Miriam to see all the different body shapes of different women—small and large breasts and hips, short, tall, round, and lanky.

The strength of the mother-daughter bond influences how girls feel about themselves and their bodies. Nowhere is this more evident than in the African-American culture, where mothers and daughters often have strong positive bonds that last throughout their lives. Beverley Jean Smith, a doctoral student in education at Harvard, discusses the solidarity between African-American women and their daughters in her essay, "Raising a Resister." Beverley said that her mother believed in her and recognized her as an individual. Once in kindergarten, Beverley kept telling her teacher that she wasn't sleepy when the teacher routinely complained that Beverley didn't take naps. Beverley finally told her mother, who then went to the school to speak with the teacher. When her mother found out that Beverley was being quiet and not disturbing anyone during nap time, she told the teacher that that was all that could be expected of the little girl. Beverley said, "From the earliest age, my mother sowed the seed of truth in me: 'Never lie to me or yourself; if we know the truth, we can deal with anything.' Mothering and daughtering are my families' acts of faith and possibilities."

A *Psychology Today* article referred to a study in which African-American girls were asked to describe the ideal girl; the findings support Beverley Jean Smith's experience with her family. Girls told the interviewers that "the ideal girl is one who has a personal sense of style, who knows where she's going, has a nice personality, gets along well with other people, and has a good head on her shoulders." Only if pushed did African-American girls name physical characteristics: fuller hips, large thighs, and a small waist.

On the other hand, white teenage girls in the same study painted an ideal girl image of Barbie: 5´7″, between 100 and 110 pounds, with blue eyes and long, flowing hair. Of the white teenagers, 90 percent told the researchers that they were dissatisfied with their weight, whereas 30 percent of the African-American girls were dissatisfied. But, the researchers noted, as black girls become involved in previously white corporate America, where a smaller body shape is desirable, concern for size starts to surface in them as well.

The Barbie-doll, fashion-model-thin ideal has led to self-starvation in many American girls and women. One of the major reasons women smoke, in spite of the dire consequences of lung cancer, is that they fear being fat; and many girls begin smoking to control their weight. Cigarette companies capitalize on their vulnerability by making "slim" cigarettes and gearing their advertisements to thinness. Obviously, this cultural ideal is seriously destructive to girls' health and self-esteem. It makes girls afraid of their bodies, of taking up space, of making themselves visible. In psychotherapy, women who are coming into their own often voice the fear that they are becoming too large, too powerful for the people around them.

You can begin to change this cultural bias for girls. Ensure your daughter's physical self-confidence by supporting her unique body and its needs from birth and give your daughter a lot of body affirmation that begins with touch. Adrienne, now the mother of two girls, told me about a nurturing, informal ritual that she has always done with them. Adrienne and her daughters go to visit Grandma Jo, Adrienne's mother, who lives a couple of hours away from their home. At Grandma's house, one girl sleeps with Grandma, the other with her mother. Each girl is given a back scratch before she falls asleep. Over the years, this intimacy that involves pleasurable, loving touch has been a ritual in their lives that shows unconditional love. When in turmoil, the older daughter, Anne, now eleven, sometimes asks her mother to scratch her back at bedtime. It is a bond between them, a way to reconnect after any kind of friction, a way to center and ground in her body.

Her body is the seat of a girl's self-esteem. If she feels comfortable in her body, she will be able to speak out about her feelings, and she will know when her feelings are affecting her body.

When she was growing up, Victoria had a warm physical relationship with her grandmother, Sadie, who lived with her family from the time Victoria was a year old. By choice, they slept in the same room—in the same bed until Victoria was ten years old. Sadie was a giving, caring, affectionate woman who did all the cooking, gardening, cleaning, and laundry. On the other hand, Victoria's mother, Adelaide, a schoolteacher, was vitriolic, bitter, and cold. Victoria said, "My grandmother and I sought solace in one another; we cried a lot together. She didn't know what to do with her daughter; I didn't know what to do with my mother." In the face of her mother's inability to care for her, Victoria was fortunate to have her grandmother to give her the hands-on nurturing that she needed.

The Transforming Power of Touch

Depending on your daughter's temperament, some simple variations of massage may be welcome from a very young age. A two or three year old may be helped to relax and go to sleep at bedtime by massaging her shoulders, neck, and back for a few minutes. Older girls, ages five to nine, may appreciate indulging in a more elaborate version of a massage. Middle-school girls who do track or ballet may need massage for sore muscles after workouts.

Sports can be a wonderful opportunity for girls to develop a healthy sense of their bodies. But some individual competitive sports such as gymnastics and ice skating have traditionally pressured girls to resist the natural weight gain that happens at puberty. Olympic gymnast Kathy Rigby, for example, suffered from an eating disorder for twelve years. She said that there was a demand to win, to maintain a certain weight, and preserve a "good girl" image. She began restricting her diet and became bulimic. At great cost to her physical and psychological well-being, she earned the highest U.S. scores in gymnastics at the 1968 Olympics and led her team to fourth place at the 1972 Olympics. When talking about overcoming her eating disorder, she said, "I had to learn to say 'No,' to find out what I really thought and felt about things. That was difficult to do because I had left that up to my coach to do for me."

Girl athletes who resist their natural weight gain at puberty take the risk of having tired muscles that injure more easily. Their coordination and good judgment may suffer. Their menstruation is also delayed, which causes girls' bodies to lose minerals that keep their bones strong. Gymnastics and ice skating are both wonderful sports, and you should encourage your daughter to participate if she is interested. But talk to her about her coaching and pay close attention to the kind of messages that she is getting about her body size.

Since the abuses in these two sports have been uncovered, much is being done to modify the pressure on young girls that causes them to delay their development through drastic self-deprivation and excessive exercise. Nutrition is being incorporated into some of the training. But your dialogue with your daughter is the best way to assess whether or not she is receiving well-balanced instruction and training that has her whole welfare in mind, not just winning the meets. She will be less susceptible to body distortion if you have educated her to a healthy practice of eating. This includes teaching her to eat when she is hungry and to pay attention to when she is full, and giving her a nutritious selection of foods.

Sometimes the best efforts of a mother toward giving a daughter a healthy sense of her own body can have ironic and unexpected results. Ruth, now in her early fifties, who felt she was overweight as a young mother in her twenties, told me that she taught Miriam to eat what she wanted and to love her body no matter what its size or shape. When Miriam was in her early twenties, Ruth chose to change her eating habits and lost twenty pounds, prompting a dismayed reaction in her daughter. Miriam was upset because she felt her mother had betrayed the value that her mother had instilled in her—that you are fine shape! This story illustrates how sensitive body image is for women and how mother-daughter attitudes about their bodies are intertwined.

Understanding Her Body at Puberty

Helping girls cope with their changing bodies from prepuberty to adolescence can take many forms. For example, Holiday Johnson, a yoga teacher and grandmother in Portland, Oregon, uses the ancient practice and wisdom of yoga. Her class, "Standing on Your Own Two Feet," uses the power of yoga to bolster girls' inner selves as much as their outer muscles. The eleven to sixteen year olds attending the weekly program spend part of each class discussing the practical applications of yoga's restraints and observances. In discussing the principles of yogic self-control, for example, the girls focus on why it's important not to gossip or to put bad food into their bodies. When the girls do the handstand pose, for instance, Ms. Johnson might say, "If you can feel comfortable standing upside down, you can feel comfortable when your life turns upside down, too." For the students, talks about friendship, school, boys, and other topics are also an important part of the class.

A girl will be more comfortable with her body when it begins to change if she has slowly gained an understanding throughout her childhood of the menstrual cycle and how to take care of herself during her period. Much of her education will naturally come from the mother-daughter relationship over the years leading up to her first bleeding. As you share your experience of your own cycles and your changing feelings, also show her your box of menstrual pads or tampons and tell her how they are used. This kind of dialogue between mother and daughter should be matter-of-fact, in the course of things, just as you familiarize her with other intimate aspects of her life.

Be sensitive to her reactions and questions and try to meet her where she is in her understanding. Little girls begin asking questions about where they came from as early as age three or four. Your daughter may surprise you with questions about sex at a very young age, depending on what she hears from older siblings, cousins, or older children at school. Betsy, a grammar-school nurse and health teacher, told me about a day when her daughter, Melissa, was four and had three girlfriends visiting. One of the friends related that she had overheard her brother talking about "humping," and Melissa came to ask her mother what this word meant. Betsy found a zoo book that described animal reproduction to show the children. She said, "When I was sitting there with all those little girls at my feet, I felt like the woman in the Mother Goose nursery rhyme, the Old Woman in the Shoe! I think that was the beginning of my training as a sex educator in the classroom."

Some girls are interested in sexual issues early in childhood, others later. Discussions with your daughter about sex and menstruation will arise naturally as she develops each year in grade school. These are the foundation for giving her information and sharing your own experience and wisdom as an adult woman. Your openness to answering her questions frankly and sincerely and your willingness to respond to her natural curiosity or anxiety will encourage her to talk to you about her developing sexuality when she is older.

A massage ritual, in its fullness, is particularly good for a puberty ceremony because it honors your daughter's changing body. The Navajo do molding or massaging in the girl's puberty ritual because they believe that a girl's body becomes soft again at the time of beginning menstruation, as it was at birth, so that she is capable of being re-formed into a woman. The White Mountain Apache also have a molding ritual in the pubescent girl's Sunrise Ceremony. The girl lies facedown in her ceremonial buckskin dress. Her godmother moves around her, massaging her from head to toe. The older woman molds the girl as if she were a baby: She touches her eyes to make them open, and then she touches her mouth. The girl is re-created.

In puberty, your daughter is entering a time of physical, emotional, and psychological change. Her body is both the source and the expression of these turbulent changes. Celebrating her body with a massage given by a caring masseuse will help her honor the changes she is going through. Acupressure massage is done with a girl clothed; Swedish massage is done nude, using a sheet to cover most of the body while a part is being worked on. You and your daughter will need to decide what is appropriate for her and the occasion. Your choice of masseuse will play a big role; it should be a woman your daughter knows and trusts. You can always arrange a meeting in advance with the masseuse so that your girl can decide for herself if she is comfortable with her.

For a massage at home, you need a table or couch the right height for massage, two pretty sheets or soft cotton blankets, a tape machine or compact disc player for playing soft music, and some scented or unscented oil or cream if the massage is to be done nude.

Any transitional time in a girl's life is a delicate opportunity for growth, a time of heightened vulnerability which signals the emergence of a potential strength. Ritual affirmation at these critical junctures helps her cross the next developmental threshold. You can use touch to do a blessing of your daughter's (clothed) body by touching her in four or five places from head to toe and saying a prayer or invocation. For this blessing, she could be sitting or standing in the center of a circle of women, or you and she could be alone. You may use flower petals, herbs, gold or silver glitter, or simply your own loving hands. Blessing her body provides the same acceptance and respect for her body as a massage. You may also teach your daughter to do a self-blessing this way.

In the Navajo ceremony, the girl chooses a sponsor for her puberty ceremony. She chooses a woman, not her mother, for qualities that she admires and would like to have herself. Her sponsor slowly dresses her and adorns her with jewelry. After the molding ceremony, people line up to be touched and shaped by the girl. The girl is believed to have acquired Changing Woman's healing power. She uses her hands to bless men and women with aches and pains, and babies and young children who want to be "stretched" so that they will grow well. The Navajo girl receives not only the caring touch of her sponsor or godmother in the massage ritual, but also a connection to the spiritual origin of her people. What is being done to her has been done to each girl and woman back to the original woman. The object is to shape her into a beautiful, strong woman.

It is crucial for a girl to respect her body and to learn to care for herself. She needs to know how to eat healthily, to keep herself clean, to get enough sleep, and to balance time with others with time for herself alone, time doing things with time just *being*. Her awareness of self-care will give her a general sense of physical self-confidence. This will be important as her body changes at puberty and will also be critical for her early sexual experience later on. Around the time of her first menstruation, a girl needs to consciously and strongly claim possession of her body. She needs to feel her physical affirmation from within, not see herself objectified for boys' or men's desires. Girls who are self-defined stay in touch with their bodies. They will be more likely to have healthy attitudes about sex. Staying in touch means listening to all that their bodies say to them, including desire. As adolescent girls with strong identities, they will make healthier choices among the many options for a productive life that are open to them as modern women. Staying in touch will also give them healthier attitudes toward childbirth, nursing, and menopause.

Appreciating Her Body, Appreciating Food

Relating in a healthy way to her body includes paying attention to the food she eats. If she naturally develops self-control by following her appetite, a girl can then enjoy eating for pleasure on celebratory occasions for which special foods are prepared and served, such as birthdays and holidays. And she will auto-matically return to moderation in her daily eating pattern.

Although we often take food for granted in our wealthy cul-ture, food is a gift. Without food, there is no life. Girls should be taught to appreciate the essential life-giving quality of food. Women are universally acknowledged as nurturers, sources of life-giving milk for their babies, and women are often responsi-ble for feeding their families. Sharing meals should be a sacred time whenever possible; enjoying a meal together can be a com-munion, a nurturing of both body and mind. Help her develop an aesthetic sense to make mealtime pleasurable. Routinely engage her in setting the table nicely, chewing her food thor-oughly, and not rushing through meals. Your daughter will learn to nurture herself as well as others.

All ethnicities have their feast days or religious holidays on which special foods are prepared: Kwanzaa, Christmas, Chanukah, Chinese New Year, Passover, and Easter, to mention only a few. Americans all share Thanksgiving. In tribal commu-nities, women work together to prepare meals. Transforming raw food into appetizing meals is a great skill. Use these collective occasions to involve your daughter in helping you plan and cook meals which honor food appropriately. Collaborate with other women and girls on these ceremonial occasions.

Show her that you value homemaking. Have her do small tasks with you at home from a young age. This will help com-pensate for the undervaluation of women's work in the home in our culture. Vi always included her own young daughter, Sherry, in shopping, cooking, and gardening. Vi believes that Sherry's strong self-esteem as a young woman came partially from working with her mother in all kinds of ways. Participating in valued work leads to taking initiative and having pride in accomplishment for girls.

Twelve-year-old Isabel says that she loves to cook with her mother. Three years ago when Isabel was nine and her sister, Jenevieve, was eleven, their mother, Elaine, asked them for the gift of their time for Mother's Day. Elaine asked the girls to help her plant and maintain a vegetable garden. The girls agreed and the three of them planted lettuce, tomatoes, corn, eggplant, and purple potatoes. Their animals—four rabbits, two cats, and two dogs—joined them in the yard. For the past three years, they have celebrated Mother's Day in this way. In the following months, they weed and watch and harvest their crops. Then they have the fun of figuring out how to cook their bounty. This is a lovely way to share the fruits of the earth with your daughter. In gardening with your girls, you tap into a long tradition of culture that has equated a girl's body with the fertile earth.

Every celebration or rite of passage can include the element of a ritual meal, however simple, whether it be a picnic in the woods at a beautiful site, a meal under a tree in the garden, around the family dinner table, or at a girl's favorite restaurant. You need only a few ideas about what foods suit the season, the ceremony, and the age of the girl and her friends. Consider first her favorite foods. Bread, cheese, and fresh spring water shared on a mountain hike can be a feast when eaten with appreciation and thanksgiving. The emphasis should be on the pleasure and joy at being able to enjoy abundance and nurturing.

At the end of the Apache girl's Sunrise Ceremony, boxes of food are given away to the hundreds of participants as a way of underscoring the celebration of the girl's life-giving powers. In the Navajo girl's ceremony, the girl helps cook meals for the guests, often numbering in the hundreds, who are present for her initiation. One of her main ritual tasks is to help in the preparation of the *alkaan*, the ceremonial cornmeal cake, that is baked in the earth. The puberty ritual is often referred to as "making her cake."

When I was growing up, we had an extraordinary cake for all celebratory occasions. It was a rich, dense, buttery cake with creamy white frosting; its signature quality was that it was red, brick red. It was called $250 Cake. The story went that my parents had first enjoyed it at their favorite restaurant in New Orleans. Then friends of theirs had asked the cook for the recipe, which arrived with a bill for $250—a staggering amount of money in the 1940s! Whenever I helped my mother make our unique cake—the red color came from a combination of cocoa powder and rhubarb—I felt an inexplicable sense of wonder. When I got my first period, I was nearly thirteen and out came the cake recipe. This time the sense of wonder was connected to my own body and the mystery of bleeding that meant I could now one day bear a child: The cake was ever more a celebration of my womanhood.

FIVE

■ ■ ■

Haircombing: Empowering Her Mind

EVERY MORNING WHEN I WAS A GIRL, from kindergarten through fourth grade, my mother braided my long, thick brown hair. She made one braid on either side of my face and then pinned them across the top of my head, where they made a crown. I loved this daily ritual—the feel of her hands combing the tangled hair, the soft tugs that made the braids smooth, the snug fit of the braids as they were pinned with small bobby pins, just so. The result—a shiny crown with all the pins hidden from sight—is memorialized in my happy, smiling fourth-grade photograph. My mother's loving and careful hands performed a wonderful ritual of adornment, of preparation for the day. It is an intimacy that I have always treasured.

Recently, a friend of mine who saw that school photo in my home said, "This picture speaks volumes to me of a mother who really enjoyed caring for you, who believed in making her daughter pretty, and who took the time to do so. My own mother was more practical, more no-nonsense. It was 'Let's get this taken care of and get on with the day.'"

Teaching your daughter to groom and care for her hair is a way to express love and respect for her femininity. Symbolically, it is also a way to honor her mind, her thoughts, her fantasies—all the cerebral activity, right brain and left brain, that is housed in her head. As you help her wash, comb, or braid her hair, express your respect for the power of her mind. Talk to her. By listening attentively to what she has to say from the beginning, you will teach her to trust her feminine intelligence, which includes both right- and left-brain activity, her body, and feminine intuition.

Honoring Female Ways of Knowing

For centuries, feminine intelligence, symbolized by the diffuse light of the moon in which objects, ideas, and feelings are seen in relation to one another, has taken second place to men's way of thinking. Men's thinking is symbolized by the light of the sun which illuminates each distinct object by itself. Dr. Christiane Northrup has written a superb book, *Women's Bodies, Women's*

Wisdom, that discusses the importance of women using all of their capacities to understand and heal themselves. She says that men use mostly the left hemisphere of their brain to think and communicate their thoughts; their reasoning is usually linear and solution oriented. The right hemisphere of the brain, which women also use in their thinking, has richer connections with the body, so women have more access to their body wisdom.

Every mother recognizes in this model her ability to perform multiple tasks simultaneously: stirring the stew for dinner, bouncing her baby on her hip, having a conversation with her husband, and helping her second-grader with her homework. Her body and mind know how to do this, whereas her husband goes serially from one task to another. But most mothers depreciate their ability to do many things at the same time because, in a patriarchal society, this mode is not valued, although it is required of women all the time.

Logic and rational procedure are the foundations of traditional education in our culture. From preschool through college, girls are trained to think, to read, to write, to do math, and to learn academics. Both girls and boys are trained to use linear, goal-directed thinking. But because diffuse, multi-task-oriented feminine thinking has been devalued, women tend to try to fit themselves into the single-focused left-brain mode, ignoring all the rest of their capacities.

Women who try to live their lives this way often feel constricted, depressed, edited; they ignore the quiet inner voice that tells them what is right for them. The masculine part of their psyches dominates their feminine identity. Instead of trusting themselves, they override their intuition in favor of masculine reasoning. Often, women in psychotherapy who made an unwise choice for a relationship, a career move, or a job, say, "Why didn't I trust my gut feeling?" or, "I knew it was wrong for me but my rational side talked me out of it," or, "Why didn't I believe the voice that whispered *no*?" These and many other women have grown up to believe that the male way of thinking, the rational way, is the right way.

Mary Field Belenky and others discuss women's body-based intuition in their book, *Women's Way of Knowing*. They describe it as a "subjective knowing" rather than the "objective knowing" of reasoning. They found that as a woman becomes aware of her inner resources for knowing and valuing, she begins to listen to the "still small voice" within her and finds an inner source of strength. They believe that a woman's growing reliance on her intuitive processes needs to happen in order for her to be able to protect, assert, and define herself; to become her own authority.

The authors also found that older maternal figures were important for a woman developing this strength. By sharing her reactions to her children, her problems with her husband, or physical complaints with a sympathetic woman who has had similar experiences, a woman starts to recognize her own experience as valuable; she too can know things. Women learning to trust their subjective knowing discover that firsthand experience is a valuable source of knowledge. They begin to feel that they can rely on their experience and "what feels right."

Feminine intuition has a central place for women. It is a flash, a *knowing* that comes unbidden, irrational, non-sensical. Women identify it in many different ways: a sixth sense, a hunch, an instinct. Emma remembers being at a party when her toddlers were aged two and three. She was chatting animatedly with someone at the top of the stairs while the girls romped around, delighting all the guests. Suddenly, in the middle of a sentence, Emma put out her arm and stopped her two year old from tumbling down the stairs. She had neither heard nor seen her daughter coming. She just knew. Many mothers have the experience of knowing that their child is crying in another room, even when they cannot hear her. Some women are suddenly aware of needing to call home when they are out, because they sense that their child needs them. A woman's intuition can contribute not only to good mothering but also to her work in the world, for example, as a real-estate agent or a human resource officer in charge of hiring.

It is time for women to reclaim their intuition, their "body knowing"; we exercise male reasoning all too well. As mothers and other women who care for girls, we need to not only become aware of our own intuition but to cultivate it in our daughters. Teach your girl to honor her body-based knowledge that includes her mind and heart and emotions.

Pay attention to your daughter's dreams. They can be a wonderful intuitive source for her self-knowledge and for your understanding her. Elizabeth's mother, Jeannette, belongs to a small women's dream group that sometimes invites their daughters to join them. Six women and three girls come on mother-daughter night, where they discuss the girls' dreams as well as some of their own. Jeannette has always worked with Elizabeth on her dreams.

Listening to your daughter's dreams and thinking about what they mean is a good way to exercise your intuitive thinking skills and help her develop hers.

During a difficult social crisis at school for Elizabeth, Jeannette dreamed that she was having a conference with her daughter and the teachers. They were all sitting at a table, discussing the problems. Suddenly, a kerosene lamp sitting on the table tipped over, and burning oil fell on Elizabeth's hand. "I did the only thing I knew to do," Jeannette said. "I quickly moved the burning oil from her hand to my hand before trying to put it out." This dream was an intuitive picture of the out-of-control situation that told Jeannette she had to take on the problem—the pain—for her daughter in order to solve it.

In our relationships with our daughters, we are often called upon to take on their suffering in order to help them. In the myth of Demeter and Persephone retold in chapter 2, Demeter's profound depression at the loss of her daughter mirrors the grief that we know Persephone is experiencing in the underworld. Demeter's grief bears fruit when she finds out who took her daughter and negotiates with Zeus to have her returned to her mother for part of the year. Jeannette was able to apply her rational skills to solving the school dilemma, but the insight came in her dream.

Brushing Her Hair, Stimulating Her Mind

Stimulating your daughter's mind begins in her early years. Hairwashing and haircombing are intimate feminine rituals that also begin when your daughter is very small. When you wash and comb her hair with love and attentiveness, you teach her self-nurturing. The act of brushing your little girl's hair before bedtime, for instance, instills in her an appreciation for taking care of herself and for winding down before sleep. When she's in grammar school, combing her hair in the morning is a good time to ask her if she remembers a dream, before it gets lost in the press of the day's events. Or perhaps she needs to go over her spelling words or her addition/subtraction flash cards to prepare for the weekly test. In these simple ways, you establish a deep connection and honor your child's lively mind.

Throughout history, hair is a symbol of feminine power. Medusa's hair turned into snakes in ancient Greek mythology, as an expression of a feminine charisma that men felt threatened by. Women in psychotherapy often dream about their mothers doing their hair. Sometimes a woman dreams that her mother is criticizing her for her hair being too long. Other times a woman dreams of her mother combing or braiding her hair or giving her a home permanent. These dreams are accompanied by a feeling of nostalgia for her girlhood in which hairdressing times with her mother were warm and related. If her mother was impatient and rough with her tender scalp, a woman remembers how it hurt her head. Usually, a mother who was inattentive or critical of her daughter's hair was also competitive with, or unappreciative of, her daughter's ideas and intuitions.

Ten-year-old Brigid has always loved letting her hair grow long, but she hates to brush it or to let her mother, Jean, do so, even when it becomes hopelessly tangled and matted. It is a source of ongoing conflict between them. Brigid knows that her hair needs to be combed if she wants to wear it long, but that doesn't keep her from struggling against it. Jean says that her big task has been to not take out her frustration on her daughter when they reach an impasse. The solution that Jean has hit upon is that in the morning when Brigid likes to play the piano, her mother stands behind her and very gently works the knots out of Brigid's fine hair. Engrossed in her playing, Brigid succumbs. Jean has found a satisfactory way for both of them to deal with the problem.

What are your memories of your mother doing your hair? Was she gentle and admiring of you? Did she spend time washing, combing, and styling your hair? Or did your grooming take second place to hers or to her work or to her getting the chores done? How do you feel about your hair now? What are your own rituals for taking care of your hair?

Rose describes her hair as always being thin, wispy, and stringy. "It brought me a lot of grief," she said. "As a teenager, I could never get up in the morning and just go out. I always had to try to work with it, prepare it in some way. I used to literally pull my hair out, standing in front of the mirror, and say to myself: Why is my hair so ugly?" Rose's mother was too preoccupied with her disturbed older son to take any time with Rose's grooming.

When her daughter, Daria, was about four years old, Rose decided to make hair ornaments, both for Daria and as supplementary income for herself. She made marvelous bows and headbands of bright, multicolored grosgrain ribbons, pale silky

French ribbons, and beaded combs. Rose sold them to friends and to local shops. It was important to Rose to do her daughter's hair nicely, and she felt healed by giving Daria what she had not had herself.

At the same time that Rose was making bows and styling her daughter's hair, she was also encouraging Daria's developing mind. Rose always supported Daria doing her homework and helped her when necessary. In middle school, when Daria showed signs of faltering in algebra, Rose took care to have her tutored. When Daria was thirteen, her mother gave her Naomi Wolf's book *The Beauty Myth* to educate her about the cosmetic industry's manipulation of women and girls. Rose wants to enable Daria to develop her own sense of herself based on her personal experience of feminine rituals.

Reclaiming Feminine Intimacy

In the early years of our country, when women's activities were more home centered, women came together to help one another dress and to braid and style one another's hair. In Louisa May Alcott's *Little Women*, recently a major motion picture, the four sisters spend a lot of intimate time combing each other's hair and reading aloud to one another. Vi tells how her mother, with four daughters of her own, instilled the philosophy of *Little Women* in her girls. Vi's mother read the book aloud, over and over, to her young daughters. "The message was," Vi said, "use your mind. Be something. Set the world on fire if you want to." Vi, a prominent family therapist with a Yale education, feels she owes her success to this early exposure to feminine nurturing and inspiring values.

This kind of feminine intimacy is often lost in our busy nuclear families in which mothers rush to get the children and themselves ready for school and work in the morning. But modern women and girls can find value in reclaiming these basic feminine intimacies. You have to choose the quality of relationship that you want with the girls in your life. The place to begin is with your own daughter or niece or godchild, who may find deep pleasure in spending time with you, trying different styles with her (and your) hair. When I lived in a small village in Greece, I often spent time in the large, cool kitchen of a fisherman's home with mothers, wives, and sisters. Even the little toddler girls joined us as the women braided my long hair and I learned to speak Greek.

Twelve-year-old Isabel and her mother, Elaine, enjoy doing crafts together. Isabel told me that one of her favorite times with her mother was when Elaine taught her to knit. Isabel's first piece was a pink shawl for her girl troll figure. A few years later, Isabel was invited to a friend's birthday party, where she learned to needlepoint; now she is teaching her mother complicated needlepoint stitches. Isabel made a needlepoint sign for her bedroom door that says "Please Come In" and a pillow with the front of a bunny on one side and the back on the other. A girl develops fine motor control doing crafts, which contributes to developing her mind.

Her Developing Identity

The way a girl wears her hair is bound up with her self-image. At some point in her early primary-school days, a girl may want to choose her own hairstyle. Choices help your daughter define and show the inner impulses of her developing identity. These impulses need only to be noticed and responded to by us as mothers, fathers, or other caregivers. As she grows older, she will want her hair to express her older self. She may cut it very short for convenience in swimming or track or other athletic activities. Or she may want it long and flowing to satisfy her fantasy of playing Alice in *Alice in Wonderland*, the school play.

Around age nine, Rose's daughter, Daria, having explored her mother's array of fancy hair ornaments, chose plainer headbands and then simple scrunchies to pull her long hair back from her face. Her mother let her make her own choices, knowing that she had given her the value of self-care. And as Daria began to separate from her mother and define herself as an individual, so did Rose. She gave up making bows and committed herself to rigorous training as an acupuncturist, a lifelong dream. Now Daria is fourteen, a freshman in high school, and Rose has just begun a private practice in Chinese medicine.

Developing girls' minds—including their intuitive skills—is critical for their involvement in the world of work. Girls' and women's traditional exclusion from the work world is acknowledged in a growing national event—Take Our Daughters to Work Day (TODTWD). Many firms have organized special group programs for the daughters of their employees on this day in April. Girls are not only able to participate in what their parent does, but also collaborate with other girls on projects that familiarize them with the day-to-day workings of, for example, a law firm, a computer company, or a theater troupe.

Lia, together with her friend Giovanna and a couple of other girls, participated in a program at Giovanna's parents' law firm. The girls interviewed each of the employees and asked questions about the work that lawyers, secretaries, and paralegals do, and about their reasons for choosing their work. They went to the courtroom and observed a session from the jury box. Then the girls wrote up the interviews and desktop-published a small newspaper. They evaluated the different jobs that they were exposed to. Lia and the other girls had definite responses and opinions about what work they found interesting or meaningful. TODTWD puts women and girls together in collaboration. It features girls in their schools and in the media, which is good for them. It also gives schools an opportunity to teach boys about sexism in the absence of the girls.

Expanding Her Mind

Take Our Daughters to Work Day provides an excellent forum for the expansion of girls' minds. But teaching your daughter to think for herself, to know her own mind, begins in her earliest years, in the intimacy of her relationship with you. We stimulate our daughters' senses as infants and toddlers with music, colorful rooms, interesting toys, and tasty foods. Stimulating her senses also influences the development of her mind. Talking to her from the time she is born, and repeating her early attempts at verbal communication, as well as reading to her will encourage her language development. In preschool, she begins to learn through play and basic work with the alphabet and numbers. Continue to share her learning experience with her. You can have her count her toys in the bathtub or count her braids in the morning. You can ask her to tell you what letters are on the cereal box. You can teach her to write her name. Your interest will awaken her interest in learning.

When your daughter goes to grammar school, continue to be involved with her schooling. As a young girl in the lower grades, she will be happy to tell you what happened to her at school that day and what she was assigned to do at home. Be attentive to her moods and her progress. Is she enthusiastic about school and proud of what she is doing? Or is she withdrawn or whiny after school and reluctant to do her homework? If you sense that she is having trouble, patiently try to figure out what is bothering her. Building self-esteem in the early years of school is important. Teach her that setting her own goals and working toward them is more valuable than measuring herself against the accomplishments of others in the class.

When she does her homework, be available. If she is in kindergarten, she may want you to sit next to her when she is doing it. As she grows older, gradually wean her from your sitting down with her. You could be cooking while she practices writing the alphabet at the kitchen table. When she is a little older yet, make a nice place in her room so that she can do her homework there. She will learn to be more and more self-reliant if you encourage her to try doing her assignments first, before asking you, and then give your help willingly when she asks.

The classroom setting is a critical environment for the development of your daughter's mind. Girls entering kindergarten are more mature than boys. In the early grades, therefore, teachers keep their classrooms under control by calling on the boys who are more impulsive, more physically active, and can't sit still. In classrooms where boys are being loud and intrusive, girls who control themselves, sit quietly, and abide by the rules suffer. Listen to her stories about what goes on at school. As she matures, discuss with her issues of gender inequality that arise in the classroom. If she complains that the disruptive students are shouting out the answers, help her problem-solve ways she can handle her frustration.

If, in middle school, she is being sexually harassed by boys on the playground, take strong measures to help her protect herself. A conference with the principal with both of you may be appropriate or you may want to talk to the principal alone.

Recall your own experiences in grammar school. Did you suffer from gender inequality as a girl? Was your mother understanding and supportive? Think about what would have helped you at significant times when you encountered such problems.

Becca remembers a time when she was propositioned by a married man, a friend of her family. Becca felt completely betrayed by the man's overtures. When she told her mother, Lily's response was a curt, "You must have imagined it." Then Becca felt doubly betrayed and hurt. Empathize with your daughter and listen when she tells you that something has happened that worried her.

Take your older daughter out to lunch now and then. Ask her about gender issues at school. Talk to her about your experience with career and gender. Do not condescend to her; speak to her as an equal, though at her level. Francesca, Giovanna's mother, recognizes her daughter's intelligence and independent nature. She sometimes reads to Giovanna from her legal briefs and invites her daughter to ask questions about the cases. Giovanna has developed a keen insight into legal complexities through her mother's willingness to share her work in this way. Girls need to hear women voicing and naming the gender inequalities in the culture. Invite dialogue with your daughter that allows her to develop a voice, to say what she thinks, to name what she sees, without fear of losing her relationship to you or others.

Francesca feels that following through on commitments is an important value to instill in her daughters. She also applies her beliefs by making sure that Giovanna consider carefully before committing to her own extracurricular activities. Recently, Francesca had a three-month trial that required her to work long hours during the week and every weekend. Although she came home to put Giovanna and her younger sister to bed at night, Giovanna complained bitterly about her mother not being home more. Francesca told her daughter that she had made a commitment to her work and to the people she represented and that she had to follow through on that commitment.

During the trial, Francesca included her out-of-town clients in family dinners on the weekends so that her daughters could meet them and hear what the big trial was all about. She also reminded Giovanna that when Giovanna had been in the school talent show, her mother had promised to come. Then the judge in a motion hearing had scheduled one of Francesca's cases for the same time as the talent show. Francesca called the judge and asked him to change his calendar because she had made a commitment to her daughter and could not appear at that time. The judge did and Francesca kept her promise to Giovanna. "Sometimes," she said to her daughter, "you come first and sometimes work comes first."

Whatever your job, hobbies, career, or passions, share them with your daughter. Show her that you respect her intelligence; honor her mind by taking her seriously and including her in your life. Share your wisdom with her and trust her to understand.

Find female role models for your daughter in her field of interest or talent. Deborah's daughter, Naomi, is gifted in mathematics. Deborah found an article on Hypatia, a famous Alexandrian woman mathematician, to share with Naomi. Deborah has also given Naomi the opportunity to go to advanced math camps in the Summer to encourage her daughter's gift.

Often role models for a girl's development come from within the family. Camille, now in her fifties, a doctor and mother of five daughters, had played the violin from age seven to fourteen, sometimes playing duets with her father. When Camille's second daughter, Johanna, showed an interest in the violin at the age of ten, her mother was both surprised and delighted. Camille dusted off her old violin and asked Johanna's grandfather to supplement the school's Suzuki class by giving his granddaughter lessons. After a year, Johanna had progressed so rapidly that

Camille decided to give her professional lessons. Johanna was also a highly competitive gymnast in these years; gradually, Johanna gave up gymnastics and became a violinist.

When Camille was pregnant with her fourth daughter, fourteen-year-old Johanna was practicing two hours a day and playing in concerts. Camille and her husband attended all the concerts, and Camille remembers the baby in her womb responding to the music. Once, during a Mozart concerto, the baby kicked to the rhythm, as if dancing. As a toddler, Daphne used to sit on the floor and listen to Johanna practice. Camille, seeing Daphne's interest at age three and a half, gave her violin lessons. Daphne had both her mother and her big sister to help her practice and is now on her way to following in Johanna's footsteps.

Shaina, Camille's youngest daughter, was born two years later into the same musical environment. Now every Saturday, Camille takes twelve-year-old Shaina to the conservatory from eight A.M. to three P.M. Shaina's ninety-minute violin practice is followed by a music theory class. After that, she and her mother have a nice lunch together in the neighborhood; in the afternoon, they return for Shaina's violin lesson. Camille is committed to helping her daughter explore her talent in every way—she takes notes at the lessons and gives Shaina constructive criticism. This is treasured time for both mother and daughter. Daphne and Shaina also did competitive swimming for five years in grammar school and are at the top of their classes at school. Their intellectual, musical, and physical development reinforced one another.

Encourage your daughter to collaborate with other girls on assignments and for recreational outings. As sisters, Johanna,

Daphne, and Shaina often worked collaboratively on their music, their school assignments, and their athletic activities. Close relationships with one another enhance girls' self-esteem. The gender separation on playgrounds that comes about quite naturally benefits girls; girls working and playing with other girls form a bond that empowers them to resist male dominance.

In order to go against the stereotype that says a girl has to choose between being pretty or smart, it is important to include your girl's accomplishments in planned rituals, as well as focusing on physical adornment and beautifying. For instance, celebrate her getting on the honor roll by getting dressed up and going out to dinner together. Or collaborate with other mothers in planning a group dinner for all the girls in the class who participated in the speech contest.

Hair-Dying Rites, Changing Identities

Take your preteen daughter's preoccupation with her hair seriously. As she grows up, she will change hairstyles many times at different phases in her life. It is the easiest, most dramatic way for her to change her look, to express a new way she feels about herself. You can ritualize any of these transformations. She may want a new hairstyle when she goes from preschool to grammar school, from grammar school to middle school, or from middle school to high school. Or she may return from camp one Summer, wanting a radical haircut. Time away from her parents, whether at camp or visiting relatives, will intensify her individuality and independence, and she will want to express her new autonomy by changing her appearance.

Eighth-grade girls sometimes dye their hair a succession of bright colors as they approach adolescence. Changing hair color mirrors their rapidly changing moods and expanding experimentation with who they are in other areas of their lives. This experimentation can have interesting, unexpected results. Marta, an eighth-grader in Lia's middle school, used her classmates and her own interest in hair dye to formulate a project for her science class. Marta tested to see which of four over-the-counter, semipermanent hair colors was the best. Using four swatches of hair, she tested for which color lasted longest, how the products' claims on the box held up, and how costs compared. Her testing results proved that the more expensive the product, the better it worked.

Girls like Marta who are already involved in playing with manifesting their changing identities will be easily engaged in more formal ceremonies. For a first-menstruation ceremony or a high-school graduation party, washing, combing, or styling your daughter's hair can be combined with ritual bathing before dressing and adorning, or done as a separate ceremony. Buying a new shampoo and conditioner always adds a special touch. Native American cultures use yucca-root shampoo and a yucca or wheat-grass brush for all ceremonial occasions.

A crowning ritual, in which you and your daughter make her a flower crown with ribbons and florist wire for an event, is also fun and appropriate for celebrating. Younger girls like to invite friends to participate in the crown making and each make their own crown.

The Quinceañera (pronounced "KEEN-se-an-YEH-ra") is a coming-of-age tradition in many Latin American communities. In honor of her fifteenth birthday, a girl is presented as a "woman" by proud parents to an assembled community. The ceremony both marks a young girl's passage into womanhood and celebrates her innocence. As part of her preparation, the girl has her hair styled and chooses or has made a special crown, often studded with rhinestones or pearls. For Karla's ceremony, she chose a pink sequined ball dress and pink tiara. She was dressed and adorned in the company of her mother, female relatives, and friends who gave her gifts of a ring, necklace, earrings, and a bracelet, as well as a Bible and rosary beads. The public ceremony began in the Catholic church and was followed by a large party. Karla said, "My mother asked me if I wanted to have a Quinceañera or a trip. You can have a trip anytime. I had good grades. I had no boyfriends. I was good. This is my reward. I am very happy."

SIX

Dressing: Developing Social Awareness

WHEN STACEY'S ELDER DAUGHTER, Sarah, was five years old, her grandmother who was visiting the family took Sarah shopping. Sarah fell in love with a dress that was several sizes too large for her. It was navy-and-white polka-dotted cotton with puff sleeves, a white collar, and a red-and-white gingham ruffle with red bows at the hem. When Sarah's grandmother saw that she would not be dissuaded by the sight of her little body swimming in this huge dress, she bought it for her anyway. Sarah wore the dress almost every day well into second grade, until the dress began to fall apart.

Clearly, for five-year-old Sarah, the dress was magical; it held a feminine quality that she was trying to realize or looked forward to realizing in the future. What a wonderful thing that her grandmother acknowledged her granddaughter's fantasy, instead of insisting that she buy something that "fit" her!

In contrast, Becca, now in her fifties, remembers that when she was four years old, her mother, Lily, sewed a dress for her with loophole buttons all the way down the front. Becca, who was an outdoorsy, rough-and-tumble pony rider, hated this dress. She remembers that her mother felt hurt and injured by her little daughter's rejection of the dress.

What a shame that Becca's mother was not able to see her young daughter for who she was, instead of putting her own expectations on her. A needless misunderstanding and alienation grew out of Lily's inability to meet her daughter as she was, to recognize her. It would only have taken observing and respecting Becca's preferences, even at such a young age. Lily could have made her a cowgirl vest or pair of pants, mirroring and affirming her daughter, and receiving appreciation and love from Becca. Instead, although Lily's intention was entirely well-meaning, both mother and daughter were made unhappy.

This is a commonplace theme between mothers and daughters who become more and more estranged over time as such misunderstandings multiply and deepen. On the other hand, listening to your girl's individual voice allows you to empathize with her and teaches her to understand herself and you.

Clothes, like hairstyles, are a vehicle for self-expression, and we can empower our daughters' independence by letting them choose what they want to wear. This isn't always easy, because in dressing our daughters, we are often unconsciously playing out a personal story of our own.

When Rose was pregnant for the first time in her mid-thirties, she found herself wanting to buy infant girl clothes. Although she tried to keep an open mind about welcoming either a boy or a girl, she couldn't help but feel that her yearnings meant that her unborn baby was a girl. When Daria was born, Rose was ecstatic, and throughout Daria's infancy and toddler years, Rose clothed her in dresses with bows, ruffles, and frills.

Years later when Rose was putting her family albums in order, she saw pictures of herself as a girl and was amazed to see that her mother had also dressed her in frilly dresses. But Rose had not received the emotional nourishment that she was able to give Daria. Daria ultimately rejected the frilly clothes but she retained the love and self-nurturing value. And through her early caring for Daria, Rose both reproduced something in her own childhood and also healed some of her own feelings of loss.

When your daughter is an infant, you will choose her clothes based on what you find appealing and appropriate for a baby girl. But as she grows older, she will begin to show preferences of her own. Many girls have marked favorites in their wardrobes as early as preschool. For a girl in kindergarten or first grade and then developing in primary school, choosing her own outfits begins to be an outward expression of her individual identity and social development. Your family values will now increasingly be impinged upon or moderated by her peers' values.

Self-Expression and Social Development

Social development is important for a girl's self-empowerment, but if you do not want a daughter who just goes along with the crowd, she needs to feel that she has the ability to make changes and choices of her own, not based on peer pressure or your pressure. This is a delicate balancing act we are asking our daughters to perform—to be comfortable being exactly who they are (self-expression) and at the same time taking other people and social convention into account (social development).

The object is to be a woman who is in touch with her own needs and creativity and also considers others. Because, historically, girls have been taught to consider others first, we must be sure that we honor our daughters' individuality and self-expression. Amazingly, this development often takes shape around the clothes they wear.

If you have chosen your daughter's clothes up to the year she goes to kindergarten, you might begin to let her choose them herself now. You could ritualize this change with a shopping trip that includes her choices. I feel that a girl, depending on her temperament, should be allowed to choose some of her own clothes at as young an age as possible—it helps her develop self-esteem and her own aesthetic. Give her a choice between two or three items that fit your budget and the current needs of her wardrobe. I remember Lia at three years old knowing immediately which of two little outfits she preferred.

The everyday ritual of dressing can be fun, but it can also be an ordeal if you and your daughter have different ideas of what she should wear. If at age seven she wants to wear her favorite dress to a party and you insist that she wear the new pink dress that Grandma just sent her, you are probably in for a major battle that will glean you nothing relationally in the long run with her. Consider whether it is worth tears and a tantrum, spoiling the day for both of you. It may be more politic to admire and then hang Grandma's dress in the closet for her to select when she wishes. She may choose to wear it another time, and you'll both enjoy the party if you don't insist.

How you handle the situation is more important than any specific result. Your daughter needs authority over her own body. Perhaps you can seek a compromise by asking your daughter to wear Grandma's dress to a family event, such as Thanksgiving, when Grandma is present. If she hates the dress, either from personal preference or because the dress is hopelessly babyish, you'll both have to tactfully deal with Grandma later.

Teach your girl to lovingly educate Grandma to her likes and dislikes. We are all taught to be polite, say thank you, and be appreciative when we are given gifts. This is an important social value. But there is also value in her letting family members or intimate friends know what her favorite colors or styles are. If your daughter dislikes the dress, she could write a note to Grandma that says, "Thank you so much for thinking of me. I look forward to an occasion to wear it. For next time, just to let you know, my favorite colors are blue and green and I wear pants to school every day." In this way, your daughter learns the value of relating and of being able to express herself not only in her choice of clothes, but through making her feelings known to her grandmother or to others. Again, this is crucial for girls, because they experience a great deal of social pressure to stifle their true preferences for the sake of the "other."

You can also teach your daughter to respond to inquiries from family members and friends about what she wants for her birthday or other holidays when gifts are given. She can both be honest and give your cousin, for example, a lot of leeway, by saying that she loves to read, play with Legos and her dollhouse, and collects Star Wars figures. Gifts are carriers of meaning in relationship—appreciation, thanks, love, acknowledgment, power. A gift that is cherished by the receiver pleases the giver too. Help your daughter understand that gifts are about relationship. It is valuable for girls to learn the social skills necessary to both give and receive gifts graciously and meaningfully.

Many grandmothers who live far away from their granddaughters use gifts to establish a connection with them. Young girls intuitively form strong bonds with their grandmothers, if the older woman opens herself to the little girl.

Judith, at age forty-nine, regrets with all her heart that her young granddaughter, Myriah, lives in another state, too far away for Judith to share Myriah's growing up on a daily basis. But Judith has kept in touch with phone calls, notes, and tiny surprise packages. Together with holiday and birthday visits back and forth, these small gestures have steadily forged a devoted relationship between them. Recently on a visit, Judith brought

Myriah a dress as a gift for her fifth birthday. Myriah loved it and put the dress on immediately. But all day she kept asking her grandmother for a bow at the waist. Finally, Judith sat down and fashioned Myriah a bow because she could see how important it was to her. Her granddaughter's wish did not have to fit her grandmother's preconceived notion of how the dress should be, nor did she have to know what it meant to Myriah. Judith accepted that Myriah wanted a bow because, at that moment, a bow expressed something of her inner world, her fantasy, her feminine identity.

"Now," Judith says, "I am remembering a robe that my mother made me when I was about age ten. I want to try to sew one like it for Myriah. The robe was made of a midnight-blue velveteen material with pink pinwale corduroy sleeves; it had silver stars appliqued or embroidered on the bodice." This robe is one of Judith's cherished memories of her otherwise difficult relationship with her mother. Judith is consciously reliving what was positive with her granddaughter. And she listens to her granddaughter's requests, likes, and dislikes.

If you give your daughter choices from a young age, the two of you will spend a lot of intimate time sharing the arena of dressing. As Vi's daughter, Sherry, grew into a large preteen girl, she needed shoes over size ten. Because they lived in a rural community, Vi would periodically drive into the big city with Sherry, to a shoe store that advertised "shoes for the hard-to-fit woman." Sherry's large feet were such an embarrassment to her that having properly fitting shoes was especially critical to her self-confidence. Vi sacrificed small luxuries for herself in order to afford the shoes Sherry needed. The two-hour drive became an informal mother-daughter ritual for Vi and Sherry. It was an opportunity for long conversations, away from the rest of the family—two stepsisters and her father. And Sherry felt her special needs met and valued by her mother.

Feeling "Right" in Her Clothes

The feelings that we communicate to our daughters about dressing and grooming influence a girl's feeling about herself as female. Dressing and grooming are the outer expression of self-care. Women whom I have seen in therapy with disturbed relationships to their mothers often describe mothers who dictated their clothes, hairstyle, and behavior so rigidly that the inner impulses of their daughters were squelched. Other women had mothers who ignored their daughters need for self-expression through dressing and grooming. Both repression and indifference were reflected in the daughter's not knowing who she was or what she needed or wanted for herself as an adult.

Such a woman often dreams of her body feeling all "wrong," of not having the right clothes for a party, of wearing her mother's clothes which are too big or too small for her. She dreams of shopping with her mother, of her mother criticizing her clothes. Having the "right" clothes, choosing clothes, or sorting out which clothes are mine and which are Mother's are the most common motifs in dreams and the most common issues in life that women struggle with in expressing themselves socially through dressing.

Honoring a girl's feelings without the cultural gender bias of "girls don't do this or that . . ." begins with the earliest socialization in a family. Mothers often have hidden agendas about dressing their daughters, based on their own experience in a culture where men have the power. Some women view clothes as camouflage to hide their femininity, not wanting to attract attention. Other women treat clothing as simply functional, while still others dress to enhance their femininity. If you emphasize appropriateness for the weather or occasion, physical comfort, and, most important, her intuitive feeling of rightness in her clothes, you will be counteracting gender stereotypes. One of the issues that often comes up between Lia and me is whether her choice of clothing is warm enough for the foggy days in the Bay Area!

Your daughter will be influenced by your conscious or unconscious attitudes. If you become aware of the way that you view dressing, you will be able to let your daughter develop her own individual style. Reflect on your own attitudes about clothes. How do you dress? Why? For whom? Is it an expression of yourself or something your mother told you or a way of pleasing men?

Ruth told me that when Miriam was in preschool, Ruth wanted her to wear overalls and boots, but little Miriam preferred ballet tutus and other fancy items of clothing. They had many struggles over their differences. Now that her daughter is a young adult, Ruth realizes that she herself had wanted to wear overalls and boots as a little girl; she had found dresses confining and restricting. Ruth sees that she tried to correct her own experience through her daughter and that, in so doing, she ignored who her daughter really was. Ruth expressed the wish that she had been more conscious of this issue as a young mother in her early twenties.

Ruth's story shows that how you felt as a girl will influence the way you treat your daughter, so talk to her about your mother's views on dressing and your feelings about it when you were her age. This will strengthen the bond between you, help her define her own preferences, and remind you of your differences.

Ask the girl in your life what her favorite clothes are that you and she buy, make, or wear. Does she like bright or muted colors or pastels? Is comfort a priority or does she prefer a fancy look? Does she like long skirts, shorts, or jeans? Does she elect to shop at secondhand stores, the Salvation Army, or the local department store? If you give your daughter ample room to express herself, you will avoid power struggles with her around grooming and choice of clothing. The everyday ritual of dressing provides countless opportunities for this kind of dialogue. In this arena, you can also talk to her about the cultural biases that may arise about how girls "should" dress.

Respecting her need for individual self-expression at each stage of development includes teaching her to respect yours. Preteen and teenage girls often begin to put down their mothers for the way they look, act, dress, and do their hair. As her peer culture grows in importance for your daughter, she will feel collective pressure to withdraw from the adults in her life. Paradoxes abound in this age group: While a girl clamors for autonomy and separation from her mother, she becomes a slave to peer norms. She is becoming an individual at the same time that she may want to dress like every other girl in her group—baggy jeans and T-shirts every day. But if you have valued her choices as a young girl, she will be less likely to feel that she has to push you away in order to establish her own identity. Respect for differences never fails in our relationships with our children.

Modeling Assertiveness

The biggest gender stereotype that girls have to fight against in their social development is the pressure for them to be nice, sweet, and pleasing to others. Girls who learn to accommodate this way do not develop a solid identity and do not learn to assert themselves. You, as her mother, "aunt," or grandmother can do something about this—model assertiveness and encourage her to be assertive. The early stages of social development take place in the context of her family, where her dawning confidence in herself is dependent on her mother and others meeting her needs and loving and respecting her unconditionally. This includes listening to her feelings and ideas, taking her seriously, offering constructive criticism, and praising her frequently for real accomplishments.

When a girl begins school, her social context widens, and her feelings, thoughts, and actions begin to be judged by different standards. In school, she will be challenged to master new skills at the same time that she is learning classroom-appropriate behavior. If she has not been raised to assert herself, she may be at a disadvantage in kindergarten, not only in the classroom where boys may be dominating, but also on the playground where other children are pushing, shoving, and grabbing the ball or the swing. You can teach your daughter to be both considerate and to put herself forward in a situation where others are not being considerate. Suggest that she approach her teacher at recess or lunchtime to ask questions that may not have been answered in class. If she is being bullied on the playground, teach her to stand up for herself; if she is bullying others, teach her to be empathic.

In school, her everyday interactions at recess and lunchtime become the forum for her learning to negotiate the balance between making friends and staying true to herself. When Mary says, "Let's play on the bars," and Joan says, "No, let's jump rope," how they negotiate a decision is the beginning of their social development in the world. The girl who always gives in to the other's suggestion eventually will tend to sacrifice too much of herself in relationships, whereas the girl who never gives in will have a difficult time maintaining friendships. It is important to talk to your girl about the interactions she has with other girls and boys at school. Your interest will support her, and you will earn her trust with considered responses to helping her with age-appropriate advice. Girls who sustain a sense of healthy self-esteem during grammar school, instead of depending on others' opinions of them, are less likely to pin their self-worth on boys' attitudes toward them at adolescence.

Girls of school age will also be learning to negotiate more formal relationships with teachers, coaches, and other adults. This will require different social skills. Teach her to make eye contact and to speak in clear, audible tones, standing straight and tall. This posture encourages her self-confidence. From the beginning, teach her to communicate with her teachers. If she is shy, schedule time for the three of you outside regular school hours. Having your time and attention as well as her teacher's will make her feel worthwhile, and she will feel empowered to seek help or share herself again.

Social pressure in grammar school becomes increasingly difficult as girls enter middle school. Jeannette's daughter, Elizabeth, had a traumatic peer experience in the sixth grade at her school. A new girl came into her small class of eleven girls and ten boys who had been together since kindergarten. The new girl was tall, gawky, dressed oddly, and had no social skills. The class members taunted her and rejected her. When Elizabeth defended and befriended her, her classmates turned on Elizabeth too. The situation worsened rapidly. Elizabeth was unable to focus on her work, her self-esteem plummeted, and she cried every day after school.

After innumerable, futile discussions with the teachers and the principal, trying to enlist them to help the class, Jeannette realized that she had to find a different school for her daughter. Other concerned parents subsequently took their children out of the school because the class was deteriorating. In your discussions with your middle-school or high-school daughter about her social interactions, you will have to walk a fine line between supportive and intrusive. But, as in Elizabeth's case, there are times when your daughter will need you to intervene.

Clothes, the Media, and Broadening Her Social Conscience

Listening to the girls in your life talk about their clothing preferences will clue you in to their social milieu. You can discern the role clothes play for them. Are the girls enjoying dressing or are they using clothes for status and being competitive with one another? Meredith's thirteen-year-old stepdaughter, Cheryl, desperately wanted a pair of $100 athletic shoes. Cheryl told her stepmother and her father that everyone else had several pairs. But Meredith did not give in because she thought the price was absurdly high. She told Cheryl that if she wanted them badly enough, she could save up her allowance and buy them herself. Cheryl decided that they weren't worth that much effort!

If you feel that your daughter's values are being skewed, that she or other girls are being made to feel bad about not being able to afford certain brands, you can quietly intervene. Reorient your daughter to clothes as a means of self-expression and to new clothes as a means of self-renewal instead of as status symbols in her social group.

Listening to your daughter and her friends, you will also learn how she is responding to media influence on the way she dresses. In order to keep your girls from buying into the plastic values of mass culture, you need to be aware of the media pressure. Is she coveting a particular brand of jeans? What do you know about the way in which these jeans are being marketed? Is your girl's preteen culture being manipulated by television commercials showing female models in suggestive poses? Or is the emphasis of the ad on the action of the wearer? These are important issues to discuss with the girls in your life.

Clothes will be an area in which your daughter will probably be vulnerable to advertising. What her friends are wearing, how she is being influenced by commercials, and her social attitudes are all part of her social development. Be sure that you are part of it, too. Ask questions like, "What does this ad suggest or teach you about the role of women?" Notice and discuss with her violent acts on television and degrading advertisements and magazines. Help her write a letter to an offending channel or program. Teach her to be critical of the media at the same time that you recognize her desire to define herself with clothing.

Be attentive to whether some of her choices are based on social issues about which she is newly conscious. Perhaps she is aware of environmental problems and wants to buy things that help save the rain forest. Perhaps she is becoming ecologically committed and wants to wear only cotton and natural fibers. Perhaps she has adopted the role of advocate for the poor and takes an interest in what happens to her worn-out or outmoded clothes. If she is interested in animal cruelty or in saving endangered species, she will be strongly against wearing the fur or skin of any animal. These social concerns are part of her search for meaning in the world and should be encouraged. They will help her develop a social conscience and mitigate against the consumer values of our culture.

As she grows older, another level of social obligation will awaken in her—an awareness of her civic responsibility. Most grammar schools have canned-food drives or toy drives around the holidays; some have opportunities for groups of children to perform little plays, sing, or dance at retirement homes. As a member of the student body in middle school, she may be a student council representative or represent her school at a spelling bee or as basketball scorekeeper. By high school, community service will be part of her required curriculum.

Your daughter's social conscience will broaden as she grows older. One night Jeannette, her husband, and Elizabeth were attending a large catered party and concert. A group of homeless people, attracted by the music and conviviality, had gathered in the street outside the doors. Without telling her mother, Elizabeth collected some food on a plate and took it outside to the homeless. The caterers called the police, and Jeannette found her daughter arguing with the policemen about her right to share her food. Jeannette was both pleased and dismayed. She was worried about her daughter's safety but touched at her impulse to help those less fortunate than herself.

Since then, Elizabeth has shown an interest in helping the homeless in other ways. Jeannette has many conversations with her about the values of contributing as well as her need to be physically safe and self-possessed. Because she and her daughter have a warm, close relationship, Jeannette trusts Elizabeth to both listen to her concerns and to find her own way with her donations.

Dressing and Mother-Daughter Bonding

Mother-daughter shopping trips, whether to a garage sale or the local mall, are implicit, everyday occasions of feminine bonding. Used purposefully to celebrate the mother-daughter relationship, differences in taste and style between mother and daughter or sister and sister can also be honored. Shopping for a birthday, Christmas, Passover, or Spring dress, or for camp clothes, are seasonal rituals for mothers and daughters. Consciously acknowledged, a sense of bonding with her mother around dressing prepares a girl for the symbolic value of dressing and adorning in the larger initiations in her life. Julia, an accomplished painter in her early fifties, said that her mother always let her choose her own clothes. "And now I'm choosing clothes for her, because she is eighty-six and cannot shop as easily as she used to."

For a shopping trip, it is good to have a morning or afternoon free, without a sense of pressure about time. Be sure to establish in advance some guidelines on budget and stores to visit so that you have a nice frame established for your time together. If you can include lunch, try to make that special and leisurely too, whether at the local coffee shop, cafe, or Mexican restaurant.

Shopping together for a skirt or dress pattern can also be a pleasure. Victoria's beloved grandmother, Sadie, made all her clothes, and Victoria remembers the satisfying hours spent together, looking for thread, buttons, zippers, and beautiful pieces of material for her school dresses. Because they lived in New Mexico, every other year Sadie would make Victoria a new fiesta dress trimmed with miles of rickrack for dress-up occasions. Victoria remembers one of her favorites being white crepe with a V neck, trimmed with silver-and-black brocade rickrack.

Remember that the value is in spending time with your girl and in the feeling of renewal that new clothing can bring. If you can communicate and share the meaning with your daughter, you can avoid the materialistic trap of her wanting more and more. Where there is no meaning, the feeling of wanting can never be satisfied. But when something is done with awareness, we receive the meaning and feel content. Instill in your daughter appreciation for the things her life brings her. Teach her to be truly receptive through your modeling of appreciation and thanks.

At a time of transition in a girl's life, the first day of school, for example, buying something new to wear (whether at the thrift store, a department store, or the flea market) becomes part of her preparation for the new school year. The first dance in sixth, seventh, or eighth grade is usually another exciting time for a girl. Although standard dress is jeans and a fitted T-shirt, there were many phone calls and much discussion among Lia's girlfriends about which shirt to wear to their first sixth-grade dance.

This sense of herself in what she wears becomes acutely important when changing from girl to preteen to adolescent. Clothes are an important element in ritualizing the transition. Taking a girl to buy her first bra can be a lovely ritual for a mother and daughter.

When Jana's daughter Kate was eleven years old, Jana took her shopping for school clothes at the end of August. Kate tried on sweater after sweater, blouse after blouse, saying that she hated each one of them. Finally, Jana said, "Maybe you're feeling uncomfortable because your breasts are developing and you feel like you need a bra." Kate said, "Yes!" And off they went to the lingerie department. After their shopping was finished, Jana said, "Let's celebrate!" and took Kate to the local ice-cream parlor, where they both ordered fantastic sundaes and talked and giggled. Jana told Kate that she was remembering being eleven years old and scheming at overnights with her girlfriends about how to ask her mother for a bra, because she was too embarrassed to ask her mother outright. Then in late August, she and her mother had gone shopping for school clothes and the same scenario had occurred that had just occurred with Jana and Kate! Jana had forgotten this episode until it happened with her own daughter. As this story shows, the anticipation, awkwardness, and embarrassment that a girl naturally feels at this time can be contained in a loving way with her mother's caring interest and attentiveness.

In all girls' puberty ceremonies that I have studied, new clothes are made for the girl to wear during her initiation. The White Mountain Apache girl prepares for her puberty ceremony many months in advance. During that time, the medicine man and her godmother make her a beautiful, fringed, white buckskin dress to wear during the ceremony. The deerskin is purchased with prescribed gifts; it is sewn and adorned with beads and cone-shaped tin charms. A large beaded neckpiece is placed around the girl's neck, a white feather dances from the back of her hair, and an abalone shell dangles over her forehead. She wears high-topped moccasins. By the end of the ceremony, the dress is streaked with the ochre cattail pollen used to bless her throughout the ritual.

The Lese tribe in the Ituri rain forest of northeastern Zaire collaborates in making a special wraparound cloth dress for each girl's puberty ceremony. Men cut bark from the fig tree and pound it into cloth. The women draw black designs on the cloth and paint the designs with red, yellow, and white pigments. The girl is wrapped in the dress by the attending women in preparation for the ritual.

Adolescent group identity resembles tribal identity in that certain behavior and appearance is required for membership. Many mothers spend hours battling with their daughters over their baggy pants and shabby T-shirts, without realizing that the output of negative energy only creates more resistance in girls who are fighting for a sense of self. But it is difficult as a mother to not be concerned with how your daughter looks to other people. If, instead of trying to prevent her from joining her peer group in this way, you can say to her, "I don't quite understand why you are dressing this way, but I love you and trust that you have good reasons for doing it," she will be able to negotiate her way through all the fads and find her own individual style. Save your parental power for things that are potentially dangerous to her. If you let her experiment with her appearance in ways that are nonintrusive, you may have more influence with her on issues that are self-destructive and which really matter, such as drugs and alcohol.

Changing from old to new clothes can be used to mark a passage for a girl at any age. You can create a ritual in which your daughter wears old clothes that belong to her younger self at the beginning of the ceremony and then have new clothes waiting, perhaps after a bath. Add meaning to the act of dressing by ritualizing any significant time in her life. For larger passages such as her first Holy Communion, thirteenth or sixteenth birthday, or Bat Mitzvah, the process of choosing, designing, or sewing the dress she will wear helps to form her new identity. How she looks and feels in her dress on that occasion is the outward expression of her inner sense of self.

SEVEN

■ ■ ■

Adorning:
Meaning, Spirit,
and the Arts

FROM THE TIME I WAS A SMALL GIRL, I loved going through my mother's jewelry box. My father had sent the small oak box, lined with dark yellow silk, to my mother from Italy, where he was stationed in the Air Force during World War II. To my child's eyes, it held wondrous treasures: pale yellow mother-of-pearl beads, dark red amber earrings, Italian cameos, and a long Guatemalan wedding necklace of silver pods. I would take each piece out of the box and try it on. I performed this ritual, asking my mother to recite where each treasure came from, anytime she permitted. I remember feeling that these jewels were precious, precious to my mother and therefore precious to me.

Girls are captivated by their mother's jewelry; it is beautiful and valued—like the feminine itself. In all traditions, jewels symbolize the inner treasure of the spirit. Girls intuit their inner treasure, the life-giving potential of their bodies and spirits.

When women in psychotherapy dream about the awkward teenagers they once were, they dream not only about their clothes and their hair, but also about their jewelry. A woman dreams of a special pearl necklace being stolen; she has lost the feminine spirit and guidance that once were a girl's birthright. The gem is always powerful, magical, or spiritual in the dreams. If the jewelry is wrong or missing, the spirit is missing. As a woman regains her feminine center and begins to nurture herself, the jewel is found and she experiences a tremendous infusion of energy and a connection to a greater feminine essence.

One woman transforming in psychotherapy dreamed that she was at the edge of a deep, wide river, trying to figure out how to get across. Wading into the muddy water, she walked to a sandbar visible partway across. Looking down, she saw a single silver earring in the shape of a new moon, inlaid with coral, turquoise, and mother-of-pearl, half-buried in the sand. As she picked it up, she wondered who had lost it. Was it herself or another woman, years before? Then she suddenly realized that the river was offering it to her as a sign that she had regained her feminine essence.

Girls and women all over the world adorn themselves with jewels and metals. Celebrate your daughter's femininity with jewelry at special times in her life. It may be appropriate to give your little daughter a small silver or gold locket on a short chain as a four or six year old. You may put a tiny image of yourself, her father, or her pet dog or cat into it. Older school-age girls love to make jewelry; bead stores are springing up everywhere. Wearing multiple silver rings on each hand is the fashion for middle- and high-school girls. Multiple ear piercings are also popular.

By the time a girl reaches puberty, the gift of a particular piece of jewelry to mark her first menstruation or coming of age is meaningful. She will be able to keep it as a touchstone for the rest of her life. Some mothers choose moonstones, alluding to her moon cycle, others red stones, reflecting her blood. But a special piece of jewelry inherited from her grandmother or aunt or godmother would also be appropriate to connect your daughter with her feminine lineage. In Meredith's family, a diamond ring has been passed down from grandmother to mother to daughter on the sixteenth birthday of each girl. Meredith grew up seeing the ring in her mother's jewelry box and hearing that it would someday be hers. She gave it to her stepdaughter, Cheryl, on her sixteenth birthday. What you choose to do with the jewelry in your girl's ceremony can take many forms. In most girls' coming-of-age rituals, the jewelry is placed directly on the girl's body by her sponsor or mother: the necklace around her neck, the crown on her head, the ring on her finger.

Adorning her with jewelry has a spiritual intention in girls'

puberty rituals. The Navajo girl is dressed in the image of
Changing Woman, the most powerful Navajo deity. Her hair is
combed to hang down her back. She wears a long skirt, long-
sleeved brightly colored shirt, and a special sash. Turquoise is
Changing Woman's sacred stone, associated with the earth. An
adorning song is sung to the girl as she is being dressed by her
woman sponsor:

> Now the child of Changing Woman,
> > now she has dressed her up,
> In the center of the Turquoise house,
> > now she has dressed her up,
> On the even turquoise floor covering,
> > now she has dressed her up,
> On the smooth floor covering of jewels,
> > now she has dressed her up,
> Turquoise Girl,
> > now she has dressed her up,
> Her turquoise shoes,
> > now she has dressed her up,
> Her turquoise clothes,
> > now she has dressed her up,
> Now a perfect turquoise having been placed on her forehead,
> > now she has dressed her up,
> Her turquoise headplume,
> > now she has dressed her up,
> Now at its tip there are small blue female birds,
> > truly beautiful;

it is shining at its tip,
> now she has dressed her up,

They call as they are playing; their voices are beautiful,
> now she has dressed her up.

She is decorated with jewels,
> now she has dressed her up,

She is decorated with soft fabrics,
> now she has dressed her up.

Behind her it is blessed;
> now she has dressed her up,

Before her it is blessed;
> now she has dressed her up,

Now the girl of long life and everlasting beauty,
> now she has dressed her up.

Now she has dressed up her child,
Now she has dressed up her child, it is said.

This Navajo song, recorded by Charlotte Frisbie, reflects the girl being layered with turquoise jewelry. She becomes the jewel and the container of the jewel, fertile with life for herself and for her people. The song expresses the cherishing care that is lavished on her as she is ceremonially dressed. Imagine how a girl celebrated in this way feels about herself: beautiful, worthwhile, powerful. Girls raised like this grow to create not only children but also their own creative and spiritual children.

Julia remembers her mother, Hester, painstakingly curling her hair for parties and dance recitals when she was a little girl.

Hester wrapped the wet hair around her finger and pinned each curl with bobby pins. When Julia's hair dried, it hung in ringlets. Although it was hard for the little girl to sit still during this procedure, she loved the effect and always felt pretty when her hair was curled this way. Hester's strong aesthetic sense also played a role in her fostering Julia's artistic talent. "I can't remember not coloring or not drawing. My parents went to baseball games every weekend in the spring and took me along when I was between the ages of six and nine. Before we left the house, my mother always checked to be sure I had my pencil and paper with me to draw."

Julia also had three other women who took an interest in her creativity: her mother's sister, Aunt Georgia, an interior designer; her maternal grandmother; and her Aunt Melba on her father's side, who was an illustrator. Hester used to mail Julia's drawings and paintings to Aunt Melba, and her aunt would write to Julia about them. Julia recalls, "I loved, better than anything else in the world, receiving a new box of crayons."

As her talent blossomed, Hester bought Julia her first box of oil paints and then found a local artist to give her lessons as an adolescent. Hester also allowed Julia to follow her instinct when she was small and play in the dirt in the backyard. There, among the gnarled roots of an old loquat tree, Julia made tunnels, streets, and shelters and sculpted a city out of dirt. Julia feels this contributed to both her groundedness and self-confidence as she went off to college at the Chicago Art Institute.

Vessels of Life and Treasure Chests

The jewelry box, as well as its contents, is important to girls who sense that their bodies are vessels, holding life-giving eggs. In Greek mythology, Pandora, the mother of all women, is legendary for the curiosity that prompted her to open a box entrusted to her by the gods, releasing human ills; only hope remained. In the older legend, Pandora's box was a pithos, a large earthenware storage jar with a lid, used for preserving wine and oil. The deeper meaning of this myth has to do with a woman's body being a container for life or death; bearing and raising a child commits a woman to facing suffering. Women dare to look, dare to face, the mysteries of light and dark that their bodies' life-giving capacities impose. Pandora's name means "all gifted one." Women's creativity manifests in all arenas of life. Whether she bears children, creates paintings, or diagnoses diseases, she shares her gifts with the world.

Giving birth to a child is a miracle, the archetypal creative act. The womb, female interior space, holds the egg, the creative potential, waiting to be fertilized by seed, idea, or inspiration. Young girls relate to their inner creativity by building interior spaces with blocks, old shoe boxes, discarded egg cartons. Older girls become enamored of boxes of old letters, chests with their grandmother's old clothes, their mother's jewelry boxes. They like to open these boxes and chests by themselves on a rainy day and try things on, daydream, and make up stories about what these old objects say to them. Or they like to hear their mothers and grandmothers and aunts and cousins tell the history of these things.

Eva grew up in war-torn Berlin. Her maternal grandmother, Gertrude, whom she remembers as stern and mean, "force marching" her to the zoo and yanking her hair, hurting her head when she combed it, would sometimes have sentimental turns. Gertrude would take her little granddaughter into the back room, the room that had been Lisa's, Eva's mother, and open an old wooden chest. It was Gertrude's wedding chest, banded with iron and engraved with the date 1860 and the names of Gertrude and her husband. There, Gertrude would slowly take out the treasured items that she felt had to do with her granddaughter's becoming a woman: the fancy pink tulle dress that Lisa had worn for her Confirmation in the Lutheran church, a special pair of pearl earrings that had belonged to Eva's great-grandmother, and a black Chinese jewelry box in the shape of a miniature house with tiny doors and drawers. She would lovingly lay each item on the bed for Eva to look at. Her grandmother said very little, but to this day her informal ritual is a cherished piece of Eva's maternal heritage. Examining each item gave Eva a piece of her mother's past and an inkling of her own future as a woman.

Many women and girls whom I have talked to told me stories about such treasures in their past, hidden away in old drawers, attics, basements, cardboard boxes, and leather trunks, silent testament to the enduring value of the feminine. Jana remembers that when she was thirteen, her mother, Mona, in a quiet intimate moment, suggested that they create a special drawer in the top drawer of her little brown dresser. Mona said this drawer would be for items related to Jana's "coming into womanhood." Together, they lined the drawer with some beautiful wrapping paper that Jana had chosen. Inside the drawer they put her "brand-new, virginal-looking pink Kotex belt and some Kotex pads, in readiness for the time I would need them." Her mother gave Jana a lovely small calendar and suggested that she use it to keep track of when her period started and how long it lasted each month. This too went into the drawer, along with a pamphlet on menstruation that they had read together and some nonutilitarian feminine treasures: a flowered sachet filled with lavender, an old-fashioned lint brush with a beautiful woman's head and torso for the handle, and a decorated wooden box to fill with tiny secrets. "To this day," Jana says, "I remember that drawer, its contents, the way it smelled, and, most of all, the delicious feminine energy and mystery which it contained."

The Intrigue of Cosmetics

Containers relate to another aspect of feminine adornment that has a long history of meaning and practice for women—face and body makeup. From ancient Mesopotamia and Egypt down to the present, women and girls have delved into the mysteries of jars of face paint, tiny vials of kohl for their eyes, bottles of perfume, boxes of bath salts, and intricately wrapped soaps.

Modern girls have the same fascination with cosmetics. April remembers when she was a preteen girl beginning to baby-sit for neighborhood families, there was one house that she especially loved to go to in the evening. In that home, the mother often waited for April to arrive before putting on her makeup and allowed April to sit in the bathroom while she "made up her face." For April, this is a luscious memory of participating by watching and learning about an adult woman mystery.

As a very young girl, Vi also had a poignant experience of learning about the use of cosmetics. Her mother took her morning coffee to her dressing table, where she did her makeup, and Vi would follow and watch in silent adoration. After her mother finished and left the room, Vi would take a sip of coffee, putting her lips to the lipstick mark on the cup, thinking: My mother kissed the cup and left the kiss for me.

Having had a mother who adorned herself and her daughters, Vi was receptive and delighted when her prepubescent stepdaughter, Emily, stuck her head out of the shower one day and asked Vi what she was doing in front of the mirror. "Putting on makeup," Vi replied. That was the beginning of a feminine connection with Emily that included many visits to the cosmetic counter. Emily's biological mother had rejected adornment, so it was new to Emily to see Vi playing with this feminine aspect of herself.

In our culture, beautifying ourselves has been split from the intellect and core strength of womanhood, denying girls an identity that includes both their mental and physical prowess and their physical beauty. This gender stereotype suggests that girls who wear jewelry or makeup are not smart or strong or are "only interested in boys." That's why women who identified with the early feminist movement rejected adornment. They were raised in families where fathers had the power and were the achievers.

Their daughters wanted to be successful, so they identified with men and repudiated feminine values, including self-adornment.

Meredith, who identifies herself as a father's daughter, now in her forties, told me the wonderful story of how she did not want to give her five-year-old stepdaughter the makeup that she had put on her Christmas list. But someone on the other side of the family gave it to her. The day after Christmas, Cheryl was visiting her father and stepmother, and the three of them were going out to dinner. Suddenly, Cheryl said, "Wait a minute! I forgot my makeup," and ran back upstairs. Meredith and her husband waited with trepidation, wondering how they were going to handle the situation. A bit later, Cheryl descended wearing one fuchsia sock, one turquoise sock, turquoise pants, and a fuchsia shirt. She had painted one half of her face fuchsia with lipstick and one half turquoise with eye shadow! Meredith was relieved to see the artistic purpose to which the makeup had been put; she had no problem with Cheryl using makeup to express herself creatively and not to fit a social stereotype.

Although the rejection of adornment on the part of feminists has been ameliorated, it is still an issue for many women today, who, like Meredith, struggle with finding their rejected femininity and supporting it in their daughters. Successful professional women in all fields who identified with their fathers, in order to avoid becoming the second-class citizens they perceived their mothers to be, now seek to reclaim feminine values.

Like Pandora, such a woman is curious enough to risk opening the box and unleashing trouble in her life; she feels she has a right to know what has been stashed away. As she opens her heart and mind, she finds the hidden treasure of the feminine in herself. Eventually, she becomes woman-identified, instead of male-identified. The previously overbearing masculine element in her psyche softens and harmonizes with her core feminine strength.

In this process, a woman may dream of finding a gold bracelet in her bed after her lover has gone home, or of a mysterious man who holds her and comforts her when she is sorrowing. Or she dreams of giving a speech, wearing a beautiful gown with a crown on her head. One such woman in therapy dreamed that I had given her a pair of gold-and-silver earrings, the sun and the moon, her masculine and feminine sides.

Olympic runner Florence Griffith Joyner has gone against this gender bias with her individual style. During her races, she wears jewelry and elaborate braided hairstyles, asserting herself visually as a woman. She is a beautiful model for girls of a whole woman using all her gifts and strengths. Likewise, in her puberty ceremony, the Navajo girl runs races to the east each day, dressed in her finery, laden with jewelry.

Our girls need the psychological equivalent. Encourage your daughter to go against stereotypes that inhibit her expression of any aspect of herself or that insist on her exhibiting only one aspect. Each girl is unique and will find her own way if given the freedom and encouragement to explore her inclinations.

In order to raise your daughter to find this balance between masculine and feminine in herself, examine your own attitudes toward wearing jewelry, ear piercing, and makeup. Do you come from a family in which piercing a baby girl's ears is a routine procedure within a few months of birth? Or do you feel that this is a decision your daughter ought to make when she is older, maybe at twelve or thirteen as she enters adolescence? Perhaps you feel she ought to wait until she is an adult. How do you feel about multiple ear piercings? Or other kinds of body piercings, such as the nose or navel?

These are questions you will probably be confronting as the mother of a preteen or teenage girl. Being prepared by knowing what your position is and being able to handle it in a way that will be mutually satisfactory to you and your daughter is very important.

In our culture, by the time a girl reaches middle school, her attitudes toward adornment avidly reflect her peer group norms. In this preteen age group, makeup, lipstick, and nail polish are explored, adopted, and discarded at dizzying speed. Many girls spontaneously create their own rituals, not only by dying their hair bright shades of red, pink, or violet but also by getting multiple ear piercings.

Any of these alterations in self-image can be used in a ceremonial way. In Native American and African tribes, for example, the skin or clothes of girls being initiated are painted during the ceremony with clay slip, pollen, or paints made by grinding up semiprecious stones. In the Apache girl's Sunrise Ceremony, the girl is painted by her godfather from the top of her head to the bottom of her buckskin boots. The painting and the songs that accompany it bless and protect her from all four sides. This creates a visible change on her body that symbolizes her new status as a woman.

Clearly, when an alteration to her body is painful and permanent, such as piercing, letting your daughter do anything she wants is not advisable from your standpoint. Neither, however, is it possible to simply say "no," and expect that she will be obedient. She might be, but many preadolescent and adolescent girls whose parents deny them permission to, for example, pierce their ears, go ahead and do it themselves with safety pins or needles.

This is not an optimal resolution to your difference of opinion. Communication with her that recognizes her developing autonomy is critical. Why does she want to have her ears or navel pierced? If when you were her age pierced ears meant that a girl was a "cheap hussy," a hippie, or a drug abuser, tell her that, so she knows why you object. And listen to her side—that this is routine for teenage girls today. Through your dialogue, you may change your social stereotype. How can the two of you negotiate a compromise, if need be, between your views and her wishes? Persuading her to agree to wait until she is older, then using the event to celebrate a transition in her development, is one way to compromise. When she is older, she will be making a more conscious choice and may then choose against it. Celebrating the transitions in her life will also enlarge her experience and ally you with her, rather than prompt an act of rebellion.

Teenage experimentation with body transformations have the unconscious goal of expressing a new identity and separating from the parents. When used to mark passages, for example, from primary school to middle school, ear piercing or makeup can become more meaningful in a girl's development. Again, you may give her a new piece of jewelry that you have made or bought, or a special family piece that you've been saving. You may also borrow pieces for the girl to wear in a ceremony. Whatever form her adornments take, bring in the meaning of the gifts in an age-appropriate way for your daughter.

Expressing Herself Through the Arts

Expressing herself through drama, dancing, singing, or painting scenery in a school play gives a girl an opportunity to play with changing her identity, creating fantasy, and varying her appearance and character. Acknowledge her unique gifts in this area. They are important for her self-expression and provide a foundation and form for the development of her feminine aesthetic and creativity.

Help her find her own creative outlets instead of subtly pushing her into activities that you think are appropriate. If her activities are self-chosen, they are beloved, ready-made channels through which she will comfortably move into creative expression. If she hates ballet and piano and she has to do them, she will not only abandon them as soon as she can, but she will spend years undoing the emotional conflict that she developed in being forced to do something that is against her nature.

Watch and listen to your daughter. Consider not only her talents but also her personality. Dramatic arts are collaborative activities; fine arts such as painting or sculpture or singing are individual. Does she gravitate toward group activity or prefer to express herself in more concentrated time alone? And, above all, what does she do that brings her joy?

Fourteen-year-old Jenevieve loves to sing. She began taking singing lessons when she was twelve, anticipating the eighth-grade play at her middle school. Jenevieve's talent blossomed when she sang "The Rose" at the school's Winter concert. Alanis Morisette is her favorite singer and role model; Jenevieve finds emotional support in her lyrics. She and her mother, Elaine, have always had a mutual love of music. Elaine took Jenevieve and her sister, Isabel, two years younger, to many local musical performances including *Les Miserables* and *Phantom of the Opera*. Now Elaine is learning to like Jenevieve's music and is earning kudos as "the coolest mom" for being interested in it and letting Jenevieve and her friends play their music loud in the car. When your daughters are teenagers, find avenues to join them in their teenage culture. This will keep the line of communication open between you.

Drama gives girls an opportunity to try on new identities in a safe context. In the eighth-grade play, she may have an opportunity to become a character that is very different from who she is in her everyday school life. If she is a quiet, studious girl in her classes and she plays the ship's flirt in *Anything Goes*, she is likely to earn new respect from her peers. And she will feel an enlargement of her own personality, an infusion of energy from expanding her sense of self.

The issue of beauty, of being pretty, often comes up in middle school. Girls who previously took their attractiveness for granted suddenly begin to compare themselves to other girls and to pay attention to other girls' criticism.

One way to explore the issue of beauty with your daughter is to look at art history books or visit an art museum together. As you look at the paintings and sculptures of women, talk about how women are portrayed in different cultures in different centuries. Is a woman or a girl in the painting elaborately made up, adorned with jewelry and embroidered clothes, as in Francisco Goya's Little Princess in the Spanish court of the eighteenth century? Or is the female figure nude, winged, triumphant, as in the Greek marble statue of Nike, the symbol of victory? Or is she a girl, perhaps seven years old, wearing a long pink dress while sitting on a garden bench and leaning on her mother's lap, as in Mary Cassatt's impressionist painting Augusta Reading to Her Daughter? Or is she an infant girl with her young mother gazing at her, as in Berthe Morisot's nineteenth-century The Cradle? Or a five year old in her mother's embrace, as in Marie-Louise Vigée-Lebrun's The Artist and Her Daughter Julie? What is suggested by each view of the girl or woman?

The more female images from different cultures that your daughter sees, the more relative her concept of beauty will be. Mexican artist Frida Kahlo painted colorful depictions of her friends' daughters. Investigate the female artists of your own ethnic heritage. Keep an eye out for gallery exhibits that feature women or girls as artists or subjects.

Painting Her Face

Painting your daughter's face is a powerful way to change her appearance and express an inner change. She may have her face painted with colorful designs at a community fair, preschool party, or birthday party. The charm of face painting lies in changing how a girl sees herself. She can become a bunny or a cat or a constellation with her own moon and stars. If she shows interest in painting as an expression of her creativity, she will be all the more intrigued by painting her face.

Celebrating entering kindergarten could include an initial visit to the school with your daughter, introducing her to her new teacher, familiarizing her with the classroom and school grounds, and returning home to have lunch. You could ask her about her feelings or impressions, then paint her face with designs of her choice. With or without discussion, your mutual participation would mark the change, the maturation, she is being called on to make. It would summon her inner resources on behalf of her own development.

The passage from fifth grade to middle school would call for a more elaborate version. In some girls, physical changes are already taking place in fifth grade; hormones are changing her body from within. Help her acknowledge this change. Painting your daughter's face at this age would call for a more sophisticated treatment, but her understanding of her change or transformation would also be fuller. When she graduates from eighth grade, you could take her to a department store cosmetic counter for a makeover.

Used ceremonially, cosmetic adornment of any kind is a wonderful way to make visible the particular rite of passage that your daughter is going through. Adrienne did a manicure for each of her daughters, Anne and Audrey, at age ten, when it was her turn to accompany her father to a fancy father-daughter dance. She wanted to support both them and her husband, and help prepare each daughter for her evening and share making herself pretty as a feminine value. Both girls felt appreciated and good about themselves on the special night with their father.

At some point, your daughter will want to experiment with using makeup on her own. She is looking for ways to express the woman she is becoming. Her experimentation will probably begin with her peers, other girls her age, often on an overnight. But you might want to arrange an hour or two alone to help her with some light makeup or take her to buy her first lip gloss. It is an opportunity for mother-daughter sharing: for you to tell stories of yourself at her age, and for her to relate how she and her peers feel about lipstick, eye shadow, and nail polish.

The local drugstore has long been a favorite haunt of adolescent girls, where they explore the mysteries of the variety of cosmetics that they become attracted to at this age. The Body Shop is a new draw for preteen girls and has the advantage of a pro-female political message, no animal testing for products, and T-shirts that say "Stop the Violence Against Women." The association of feminine beauty with a cause—no animal testing—that is not male driven (neither sexual nor violent), gives a young girl the possibility of exploring feminine adornment for herself, without becoming an object for men.

Again, discuss the media with her. How is makeup being advertised and for what purpose? Discuss how women look on television and ask why. Do they look like objects for men to look at? Or do they look as though they are pleasing themselves?

Encourage your daughter to please herself!

You may use face painting or makeup as the central motif of a group ceremony for your daughter and her friends. It could be an end-of-the-school-year party or a beginning-of-the-school-year party. Tell each girl in advance to think of the designs she would like to have drawn on her face; her chosen designs will be the center of her activity at the party. Have old clothes, scarves, and jewelry available for dressing to amplify their painted faces. You and your daughter could also ask the guests to bring bits of costume to amplify their own symbols.

At the party, painting one another's nails as well as faces might be included. Then each girl may write a short story about the person or element (star, moon, and so on) that she chose to embody and share it with the other girls in a storytelling circle. Or the girls together may create an impromptu drama to enact for you (and other mothers or adults) at the end of the party. This is a terrific creative experience for girls. It both honors the girls' individuality and helps them create community. It emphasizes their talents as girls in a supportive, noncompetitive environment of fun and challenge.

Mother-Daughter Beautifying

From the time Daria was ten or eleven, when her skin began to show hormonal changes, her mother, Rose, has given her herbal facials about once a month. By creating a nurturing ritual of steaming, cleaning, and applying a masque to Daria's face,

Rose has taught her daughter how to take care of her skin. When Daria graduated from eighth grade and, more recently, the first week of high school, her mother gave her a gift certificate for a salon facial. This is a lovely way to honor your daughter's changing body and chemistry and help her learn to take care of herself. It can also be a nonintrusive way to help your girl address her embarrassment with the signs of change that her skin is showing. If she is too uncomfortable with you, there are many skin-care specialists who have reduced prices for teenagers.

Surprise her with an idea for beautifying one another on an evening when the two of you are alone, when the rest of the family is occupied or out of town. Have a box of face paints and several small brushes of varying widths, or an array of cosmetics, a facial mask, or flower pollen (the stamens of pollen-laden flowers such as lilies). Combine the painting with beaded-jewelry making or some other craft. Remember, this intimate time together focusing on her and/or your adornment is nurturing her feminine spirit. Even if you do not talk about it overtly, the symbols of jewelry and containers and makeup will influence her psyche and her soul.

At every passage—birthday, starting a new level of school, losing teeth, beginning a new sport—a girl's talent and interest in music, art, drama, or movement can be engaged in designing a celebration. Involving your daughter in designing a ceremony with her individual gifts and personal accomplishments will bring her into her femininity in a whole way. If she begins at a young age and her creativity has been fostered, her involvement in ritual will develop naturally and grow as she grows. She will gradually collaborate with her parents or other adults and friends in creating meaningful passages, culminating in shaping her puberty ceremony. If she is introduced to it later, the meaning and power of such ceremonies will engage her.

A five-year-old girl may draw pictures with which to decorate the kitchen for her birthday party. An eight year old may help in planning her party and selecting the theme, the activities, and the favors. A preteen girl may enjoy designing a scavenger hunt that tells a story about herself and includes beads or jewels, makeup, and natural treasures such as stones, shells, and leaves.

For my daughter's ninth birthday, she had a jewelry-making party. We bought plastic beads of all colors, shapes, and sizes and an El Salvadoran parrot bead for each of her friends. The parrots complemented Lia's chosen tropical theme. For three hours, nine girls sat busily making necklaces, anklets, and earrings from the materials at hand. Whatever the girls made, they kept as favors. After drinking punch, eating strawberry-cream cake, and Lia's opening her presents, we took them to the local swimming pool where they swam and dove for two hours, before being picked up by their parents. This birthday celebration involved several elements: making jewelry, celebratory food, gift giving, and physical empowerment. Each girl was able to be creative and to adorn herself or a friend with the jewelry she had made. Everyone shared in celebrating Lia's special day. And they reveled in their strong young bodies with swimming. The day was a well-rounded experience for each girl.

EIGHT

■ ■ ■

Storytelling: Teaching and Learning

RECENTLY, LIA WAS STUDYING early Mesopotamian civilization. Although several pages of her world history book were devoted to King Sargon of Ur, there was no mention of his renowned daughter Enheduanna, the first recorded poet-priestess of the world. The minor god Nann was mentioned, yet the chief Sumerian deity, the moon goddess Inanna, was omitted.

As I told Lia about Enheduanna and Inanna, her eyes grew big and she exclaimed, "What? That's not fair!" We decided to write up a page on Enheduanna and Inanna for her history teacher, Polly, so that the class (two-thirds girls!) could hear about their ancestress.

The omission in Lia's history book reflects how male oriented our culture has been; our history has been written by men, so many of our cultural heroines have been lost. Traditional education focuses on famous or talented men with almost no mention of important women or female religious figures. Therefore, we must embrace the task of teaching our daughters about the feminine history that makes up our mother-daughter lineage from the beginning of time.

Our understanding of this rich history can also enhance us as adult women and increase our self-worth, as we see ourselves as part of a long and important tradition. And once we begin to look, we do not have to reach back thousands of years to find our cultural heroines. Many contemporary women in the public arena as well as our grandmothers or great-grandmothers, aunts, and cousins make worthy models for our daughters.

One way to introduce your girl to important female role models is to include someone you admire in a family ceremony. For example, for the African American holiday Kwanzaa, celebrated between December 26 and 31, a child lights a candle on each day to honor a quality that is important for her people. On one day, the quality celebrated is creativity. You could have your daughter light the candle that day and read to her from U.S. poet laureate Rita Dove's latest volume of poems, *Mother Love*. Or you could tell her about Nobel prizewinner Toni Morrison's life and work.

Storytelling is naming. It puts words to our experience, our feelings, thoughts, actions, fantasies. It is a wonderful teaching tool because it involves both the teller and the listener in mutual participation. Stories makes sense of our lives. In telling stories to our daughters we name our own desires and dreams. Simultaneously, we are giving them permission to name theirs and teaching them a vocabulary for naming feminine experience. Who have been your heroines, women whom you have admired or found inspiring? Are they women explorers or high-powered businesswomen? Have you found comfort or spiritual awakening in relation to a goddess or female divinity? Share the stories of your ancestresses and female idols with the girls in your life.

Usually, it is the women in families who have kept alive the traditions and customs of their tribes, nationalities, and religions. Women have traditionally cooked the special foods for Christmas or Passover or Lent. They have decorated their homes and tended the shrines in churches and synagogues. And they have told the stories and taught their daughters how to carry on these traditions.

Telling your daughter stories about her grandmothers, or about women who have influenced you, not only gives her a sense of her origins, but also weaves the rich tapestry of the relationship between you. It gives her a context in which to view herself as a girl on the verge of the twenty-first century.

Think about the customs that you have kept alive from your family or ethnic origins and find ways to share those with your daughter. Include her in your preparations for holidays, whether it be preparing an altar and baking for the Mexican Day of the

Dead celebration in November or cleaning the house for Persian New Year in the Spring.

These preparations take on new meaning if you tell the stories of how the holiday evolved and what it means to you personally. Did you grow up with it? Or have you taken it on in your marriage or partnership and found your own meaning in relation to it? Your daughter will profit from this kind of dialogue and so will you. She will grow secure in the knowledge of who she is and where she comes from. You may find new meaning in reflecting on and telling her stories about customs you may have taken for granted. In the intimacy of your relationship to her, you may recover stories from your past that you had forgotten.

And remember, she needs to hear not only your positive, glorious stories, but also stories about your difficulties as a child and, as she gets older, as a woman. Telling her about your sadness, rejections, and feelings of inadequacy will help her deal with those shadowy moments in her own life. Then she is able to see that all lives have shadow and that you, an important woman in her life, have experienced difficulty and dealt with it.

Don't be afraid to offer some of your hard-won wisdom. It is important to tell her about how badly you felt in challenging times and about what those problems taught you. Lia says that she learns from hearing about women's mistakes as well as from our good choices. And, she says, listening to her grandmother, godmother, and me gives her ideas about what she might want to do with her future.

You will know what kinds of stories to share and when to share them by interacting with your daughter or granddaughter at her age or developmental level and by being sensitive and attentive to her needs. Your own development as a mother is also important. If you are a young mother in your twenties, you will have a different sense of life to share with her than if you are in your late thirties.

Jana feels that there were benefits to being a young mother in terms of her having a lot of energy and optimism to share with her children. But she wishes that she had had the wisdom that many older mothers have when it came to mothering her daughter Kate through adolescence. But whatever age you become a mother, you will learn from your daughter by listening to her. By your hearing her cries, responding to her basic needs, then heeding her words as she communicates with thoughts and feelings, she will learn to listen to you in all your complexity.

Sometimes, a little girl will become entranced by a particular fairy tale or book or author. This means that she has found something of her inner self in that tale. Encourage her passion, even if it means reading the same story over and over again for years. Kathryn Lasky, a Newberry award–winning children's author, gave her daughter the complete set of Laura Ingalls Wilder's *Little House* books when Meribah was five years old. Meribah's eyes would light up when her parents read the stories out loud to her. When she learned to read, Meribah read them all herself. At age twelve, she and her mother decided to visit the places Laura Ingalls lived as a child. They traveled through Wisconsin, Minnesota, and South Dakota with her father, Christopher Knight, a professional photographer. Kathryn and Meribah wrote journals on the trip; Christopher took photos.

Then Meribah and her mother returned home to Massachusetts and wrote *Searching for Laura Ingalls* in two months.

Clearly, Meribah's development has been productively influenced by her parents' reading to her. As with Meribah, reading stories to your daughter will stimulate her imagination and creativity. It is never too early to begin reading to your daughter.

From the time she can sit in your lap and enjoy seeing the pictures unfold, children's books of fairy tales and myths will give her a sense of forces larger than herself. This will contribute to her psychological development. Stories with girl heroines can also communicate feminine values. One of Lia's favorite books at age four was *Dizzy from Fools*. In this story, the king's daughter wants to be the court jester but is told by her mother, the queen, that only boys can apply for the job. The princess disguises herself as a boy, wins the contest, and only then reveals to her father who his favorite jester really is.

Choose books for your girls that show girls as active rather than passive characters, where girls initiate the action. In *Naya Nuki, Girl Who Ran*, the eleven-year-old Shoshoni girl is taken prisoner by the Minnetare Indians and force-marched from Montana to North Dakota, where she becomes a slave. Through stealth and careful planning, she plans her escape. During the long, lonely journey, running at night back to her people, she survives through her wit, daring, and skill. Her guiding beacon throughout her ordeal is her love for her mother. Weeks later, when she reaches her village, the story says, "she ran to her mother and threw her arms around her mother's neck. The tears flowed freely as mother and daughter cried for joy. It was a scene that no Indian standing there would ever forget. It was a story that would be told around Indian campfires for years to come."

Naya Nuki was both loving and brave. Books such as *Naya Nuki GirlWho Ran*, that portray girls as competent individuals convey the message that girls can be good at a variety of tasks, including traditionally male activities. Girls who feel competent about their abilities are also confident about themselves.

Books that show girls accomplishing their goals inspire girls who might otherwise doubt themselves when faced with obstacles. In *Nobody Listens to Me*, eleven-year-old Mendy, whose mother died when she was five, helps her father out on his whale-watching boat. When her favorite whale dies, she learns that whale watching is hurting the whales. She begins to campaign against her father's business by picketing, putting up posters, and handing out leaflets in her small seaside town. Many of the townspeople try to stop her. But Mendy is determined, even though she and her father become alienated. She believes so strongly in her cause that she succeeds in bringing it to the attention of national media and finally wins her father over to her point of view.

Throughout primary school, reading aloud and storytelling continue to be an important way of relating between mother and daughter. Twelve-year-old Shaina cherishes the time she and her older sister, Daphne, spent with their mother, Camille, reading the Oz books. Camille had collected many variations of the Oz stories by L. Frank Baum and Ruth Plumly Thompson. The three of them made it a project to go into a nearby city to comb the secondhand bookstores for volumes that they were missing. Shaina says that she loved the books because "they were imaginative, totally original, very fun to read, and cool. And I felt as if the magic was happening to me." After a difficult day for your daughter, dealing with an upset at school or at home, your selecting her favorite book or making up a story at bedtime can help resolve upsetting emotions and affirm the bond between you.

Strengthening Her Sense of Self

When your daughter learns to write, encourage her to keep a journal. Teach her that her journal is private, that she can say anything she wants to say. No one will see it or criticize it. Being uninhibited in her journal will strengthen her sense of self and her ability for self-reflection.

If she writes stories, listen to her read them aloud. Think about the kinds of stories that a girl writes, even for school. Morgan noticed that her nine-year-old daughter, Briana, who loved to read and write, initially responded to a creative-writing assignment with a story featuring a strong, shadowy woman character with a lot of passionate emotions. When Briana finished it, she read it aloud to her mother. Morgan said, "Wow, that's great, very powerful!" The young girl immediately crumpled up the paper and said, "I didn't want it to be powerful; it's no good!" Then Briana rewrote the story, making it lighter and sweeter. Noticing this, Morgan began to work with her daughter, a cooperative, well-balanced, charming little girl, to feel more comfortable with expressing her darker emotions. Eventually, Briana wrote stories that expressed both sides. This is an excellent example of the way in which a young girl can become identified with a cultural standard of being "good" to the detriment of her creativity and wholeness. Luckily, Morgan was aware enough to help her daughter negotiate this critical moment in her creative development.

Books can directly influence a girl's self-esteem. In the 1950s, a whole generation of young girls was influenced by Nancy Drew, the teenage heroine of more than a hundred books. In April 1993, 450 scholars, collectors, and fans gathered at the University of Iowa for the first Nancy Drew Conference to look for clues in her books about the erosion of self-confidence that girls are faced with today. "What matters in the (original) books is not her sex appeal but how tough, smart, and adventurous she is," said Catharine R. Stimpson, a professor at Rutgers University who studies women and society. "It means something that mothers and aunts give the books to their nieces and daughters. She's a legacy—a spiritual treasure passed on."

Give a girl in your life one of the original Nancy Drew books. Or find another writer who you think presents heroines in confident, competent, and brave ways to introduce to a girl at just the right age.

Sally Lockhart, the young Victorian heroine of a trilogy of books by Philip Pullman, is just such a girl. She not only fights successfully against a series of personal adversaries, but also rejects the nineteenth-century prejudices against girls and women to achieve both financial independence and an unconventional, satisfying personal life. Reading the right book at exactly the right time in her development can change a girl's life.

If you were an avid reader as a child and are tuning in to your daughter's needs, you will intuitively know which book to give her at what age. If you feel uncertain, consult the children's librarian at the public library or a knowledgeable book buyer at a local bookstore. Browsing with your daughter in the library or an inviting bookstore is a good ritual to begin early in her life.

Valuing Her Heritage

Talk to your daughter about her heritage. Were her grandparents Irish, Italian, Jewish, African American, Hispanic, Greek? These are her roots. Elements from her different ancestors are alive in her psyche; all contribute to her wholeness. The more aware she is of those elements, the more she will have access to her individual strengths. The family of Ellen's Chinese mother, Mui-Ji, is from Hong Kong. About once a month, Mui-Ji takes Ellen to have breakfast at her aunt's Cantonese restaurant; after eating, Mui-Ji and Ellen help out in the restaurant. Mui-Ji told me, "Neither of us is brave enough to take orders though; the customers speak a melange of village dialects that is incomprehensible even to me!" They wind up the day by visiting Ellen's grandparents, where she always learns about Chinese customs.

How and why did you choose your daughter's name? Little girls love to hear about their names and often ask a million questions about what other names you considered or how you liked your own name as a child. This is a story that they love to hear over and over. Periodically, a girl may say that she wishes she had been called a different name; this reflects a wish for some change in self-perception, a shift in identity, a reaching toward some new aspect of herself. Ask her what it would feel like if she were called Sabrina, or whatever her current fantasy is, instead of her given name, and you may find a delightful wealth of insight into your daughter's inner world. Most of the girls whose stories are told in this book, including my daughter, chose their pseudonyms. By participating in this way, the girls were able to play with changing identities, and by sharing their own stories for publication, they affirmed their personal experience.

Girls also love to hear family stories over and over, especially ones that they were part of. Between the ages of three and four, every night at bedtime Giovanna asked Francesca to tell her the story of when she was born. The story always began with Francesca going into labor, then what Daddy said, then what Grandma and Grandpa, who were visiting, said (Grandpa started crying), and what the toll-taker on the bridge to the city hospital said. The story progressed through labor and finally to Francesca needing a general anesthetic and waking up to hear the doctor saying, "You have a beautiful little girl." If Francesca varied the story at all, Giovanna would correct her.

Girls like to hear about their beginnings. If you record your daughter's development in a baby book when she is an infant and toddler, you can read from it to her as a kindergartner. Later, when she can read, she will pore over your words herself. She will be nurtured by the time and attention you lavished on her. Whether oral or written, you are contributing to a healthy psychological makeup in your child by sharing stories with her; they will become part of her inner resources.

Girls have a fine way of asking questions about stories that illumine areas that their mothers and aunts have not noticed. Girls are, after all, partaking in the future as they come into their own, whereas we belong more and more to the past as we grow older. Grandmothers find their granddaughters asking questions that their own daughters did not ask. Grandmothers and godmothers often feel freer to share their personal stories of defeat or triumph, or to offer a different view from the girl's mother, because they do not have the primary responsibility for their granddaughters and goddaughters and have fewer expectations. They are often magnificent influences on girls. The Auntie Mame character of the 1950s was a cinematic characterization of the godmother role. Flamboyant and extravagant, she brought a free-spirited, unconventional feminine energy into the lives of the girls in her family.

Laura, who raised two sons, now has her niece, Katja, living with her. Katja needed a break from college and from a relationship with a man to reorient herself in life. The aunt and niece now take walks together, and Laura expressed surprise and delight at how in this intimate feminine context, they found themselves talking about contraception; she told Katja about her own five-year struggle with infertility in a second marriage, grieving the inexplicable loss of children to miscarriages. Laura told Katja both about her pain and about her emergence into a different kind of creativity. Laura had not had this kind of storytelling exchange with her two sons. What a gift to Katja to be able to take time out from the ordinary progression of college to share intimacies with her aunt, to get a sense of the potential for growth hidden in life's difficulties.

The craft of quilting has traditionally been a time when women come together and tell stories at quilting bees. The quilt patterns often illustrated the female life cycle and the domestic world of women. But they also documented a record of America's history from the time of the settlement of the English colonies through the Civil War. The women who made these quilts recorded their responses to important historical events with pictures, names, and dates. For example, a quilt made around 1870, a few years after the first U.S. National Women's Rights Convention, shows appliquéd vignettes of a woman engaged in activities considered radical at the time: driving her own buggy with a banner advocating "Woman Rights," dressed to go out while her husband wears an apron, and, most surprising, addressing a public meeting.

Here we have a rich tradition of American women coming together to share their lives with one another and collaborate on a craft that has contributed to our art and our history. Doing creative projects with a group of peers has been shown to have a major impact on girls' and women's empowerment. Girls find a larger vision and are stimulated through their interaction in a framework of emotional connectedness. They experience an increase in energy and feel more effective when they use their ability to contribute to the group's success. The book and movie *How to Make an American Quilt* is a dramatization of a women's storytelling ritual done for a young woman. In this case, the girl, Finn, is a college student who can't quite settle with her commitment to marry her fiancée. She goes to the home of her great-aunt and grandmother in the country for three months to write her Ph.D.

dissertation and make up her mind about her boyfriend, Sam. While she is there, the older women invite their quilting group to sew her a wedding quilt with the theme *Where Love Abides*. As each woman makes a square for the quilt, she remembers her own life, which we see in flashbacks. The choices they made about themselves and their marriages have consequences in the present. In other words, they come together to share their wisdom with the young woman.

The movie is interesting on two levels. Winona Ryder plays the part of Finn, and the older women are played by mature actresses who have lived rich complicated lives. During the making of the film, Winona Ryder must have been learning about acting from the older women as well as playing a part in which she ostensibly learned about love.

Movies and television are a big part of girls' peer culture. Whether it is for younger girls or older girls, *Pocahontas, Beauty and the Beast*, and *The Secret Garden* all convey a message about being female. Matter-of-factly monitor what she sees by finding out with her in advance what a movie is about. Then see the movie together and discuss it afterward. Help raise her consciousness about the roles women play in films. Older girls seeing movies like *Thelma and Louise* or *The Piano* will be exposed to powerful feminist messages. Ask her about her responses; share your perspective with her. If, as a typical adolescent, your daughter does not want to go to the movies with you, go separately with your husband or a friend so that you can still discuss it with her later; or rent a video together and spend a cozy night at home, watching and talking.

Violence and degrading sexuality in movies and on television is routine. These media have the power to shape reality in both positive and negative ways for our daughters. The way women and girls have been traditionally portrayed—either as perfect homemakers or artificial sex symbols—has had a harmful influence on girls.

To address this problem, Girls Incorporated, a research and advocacy group devoted to helping every girl become "strong, smart, and bold," launched Girls Re-Cast TV, a national media literacy and advocacy campaign that teaches girls to evaluate what they see and hear on television. Based on the fact that young people watch an average of twenty-one hours of TV every week, thousands of females in grades three through twelve wrote to television executives and told them what they think of the way girls are portrayed on television. Isabel Stewart, the national executive director of Girls Inc., said "Girls want to see more realistic images of themselves, while boys want more of the same—sex, drugs and violence. The ultimate goal is to put today's girls not just on TV but in network corner offices." In the poll, the girls said that they wanted girls and women on TV to have more adventures, more interesting careers, and come from diverse ethnic and racial groups.

The stereotypes of women depicted on television do not reflect girls' lives. The Girls Inc. media literacy curriculum helps girls explore some of the subtle and overt messages sent through the media and teaches them ways to channel their opinions into creative action. Girls learn to create their own characters and recognize stereotypes; they are given the chance to rewrite scenes from popular sitcoms, develop their own music video story-boards, and determine their own rating system for the shows they love (and hate) to watch. The fewer number of hours of TV watched, the more likely girls were to create TV shows about females who are athletic, good leaders, concerned with friends, sensitive to the needs of others, and who aspire to be leaders. The more TV girls watched, the more likely they were to create a female main character who is rich and thin; concerned only about popularity, clothes, and money; and who aspires to be a model or movie star.

Therefore, monitor your girl's TV programs and watch them with her sometimes. Talk with her about how women and girls are portrayed and ask her questions. Who is her favorite character? Why does she like her? How are the character's behavior and reactions similar to or different from her own? She will develop critical thinking and psychological acuity that she can apply to other programs and movies that she sees. You will be helping her to define herself as an individual and to not succumb to media propaganda.

Mother-Daughter Conversation

These are the kinds of intimate conversational interactions our daughters need at all stages of their lives. They teach them what they need to know about their own bodies, their own beings; they teach them the value of relationship with other girls and women; they help them be secure in themselves. They allow the two of you to know each other. Such an upbringing will enable girls to be more assertive in their relationships with men and in their work and careers because they will know themselves.

Instruction through the mother-daughter relationship occurs through both actions and words. Telling stories is a good way of imparting values, information, and subtle feminine mysteries. This will happen naturally in the course of raising your daughter if you allow some downtime with just the two of you alone. Young girls enjoy going through your photograph albums and hearing about your experiences over the years. Judith plans to make a family scrapbook for her granddaughter Myriah as part of her legacy to her. Video cameras have also become a popular way to record the events in children's lives. Reviewing herself at a younger age gives her a solid sense of her own individual history.

Our feminine history can be conveyed in the everyday inter-actions between women and girls that occur while playing soccer, driving to Girl Scouts, or back and forth to school. In these ordinary moments, we are modeling the adult women our daughters will become. We are informally teaching our daughters attitudes and values about their bodies, their minds, and their potential roles in society. We can also convey the essence of womanhood in more formal ways.

All traditional puberty ceremonies involve some education about the girl's growing up. Storytelling is important to these ceremonies. The Navajo girl is instructed on her new responsibilities as a woman through stories about Changing Woman, whereas the girl of an Amazon tribe ritually enacts the adventures of three mythic heroines who serve as teachers for her.

Storytelling becomes a more formal ceremony if you plan it to include other women and girls. You may do this for a girl's birthday as early as age eight. It is also wonderful to incorporate into a coming-of-age celebration, because there is much wisdom to share with a girl who has just begun to menstruate.

For a storytelling circle, honoring one girl, it is nice to place the girl in a special seat/throne at the head of the room. The guests then sit in a semicircle around her. You might want some soft background music, but nothing that will detract from the voices of the women and girls as they speak. It is always fun to collaborate with your daughter on invitations that reflect her feelings about herself on this occasion. If it is her eighth birthday, she may want to hand-draw bubble letters. If she is thirteen and has just begun menstruating, she will probably choose to buy cards with a more complex symbol.

You may ask each woman and girl to tell a story about herself when she was your girl's age or to give her a wish or blessing. In the fairy tale *Sleeping Beauty*, the king and queen performed this ceremony to welcome and bless their daughter at birth. In the story, twelve fairies offer good wishes, but the uninvited thirteenth fairy crashes the party and wishes the long sleep upon Sleeping Beauty, at age sixteen. One moral of this story is that we should always include the shadow, because it comes into our lives anyway.

This means that although most of the stories told in your group would be loving and sweet, others could include something serious or painful, appropriate to the girl and the occasion. With a younger child, the shadow is often expressed through humor or teasing. At a party for an eight-year-old girl, an amusing story about an embarrassment at that age or offering a favorite book from that age would be appropriate. For the newly menstruating thirteen year old, it could be a story from a guest about her first period or other feminine experience that she wishes to offer the honored girl.

At one coming-of-age ceremony that I attended, one of the women in the circle brought up the shadow by speaking of her pain at not having been celebrated when she began menstruating. She said that this ceremony was healing for her own loss; it made her happy to celebrate the young woman. Many women express both feelings of loss at not having had feminine rituals as they were growing up, and of joy and healing at finding ways to celebrate girls and themselves as adult women.

It is nice in a storytelling circle to have a special stone or talisman that carries the energy of storytelling for you. Many Native American tribes use a peace pipe, a storytelling stone with the image of an animal engraved on it, a bowl of cornmeal, or a talking stick. The stone or bowl or stick is passed to each woman and girl in turn as she speaks. Its purpose is to provide inspiration to the storyteller and to remind the others to stay silent; unless you are holding the object, you may not speak. You may introduce the circle celebration by using this object to explain why you are all there and what your chosen talisman means for you or your daughter. You may either begin with your own story to open the circle or wait to be last to complete the circle. When everyone is finished, your daughter may wish to say something she has prepared, or she may respond spontaneously to the group, or she may say nothing at all. Afterward, when everyone adjourns for cake and ice cream, refreshments, or a meal, the girl will feel truly seen and acknowledged at this passage in her life.

Spreading the Feminine Word

A single affirmative act between a woman and a girl, on behalf of the feminine, ripples out to larger and larger groups of girls and women in our culture. My daughter's and my discussion of how the important women leaders in Mesopotamia had been left out of her history book happened in our intimate everyday time after school. It came out of my experience in a women writers' salon in which Enheduanna's poems were read. Writing up a page on this first woman poet of the world for Lia to take to class celebrated the feminine not only for Lia, but also for her teacher, Polly, her sixth-grade peer group of both girls and boys, and, hopefully, for future sixth-grade classes in her school.

Polly was delighted to receive the information and told me that when the class played "Who's Who in History?" she always began the game herself by naming a woman historical figure. Obviously, Polly is honoring the feminine in class, correcting for the male gender bias in history books. Perhaps she also shared her new knowledge of Enheduanna with other sixth-grade teachers at their annual teacher's conference, and the ripple of female affirmation continues to spread.

NINE

■ ■ ■

Strengthening Her Body: Sports and Menstruation

M EREDITH WAS AN UNCONDITIONAL FAN of her stepdaughter Cheryl's sports. Together with Cheryl's mother and father, she went to all her volleyball games. Cheryl was strongly internally motivated and always pushed herself to live up to the coach's male-defined standards. Meredith found herself being the advocate of a more feminine attitude for her stepdaughter. Meredith encouraged Cheryl to take care of herself and not to push herself past her body's limits, values that her male coach had called "sissy." Once, Cheryl told Meredith that the coach had accused her of not having enough "heart" for the game. Upset by the implications of this comment, Meredith assured Cheryl that "heart" was not her problem, but that the coach was trying to force her to play beyond her body's comfort zone. Because of his relentless pushing, Cheryl did exceed her limits and ended up with two stress fractures in her legs.

As Cheryl's story illustrates, girls need women to support them both to do sports and to do them without giving up feminine values of nurturance and support. Traditionally, girls have not been encouraged to be physically active, and stereotypes of girls not playing sports are still rampant. Female athletes are not featured as often as male athletes by the media, especially for team sports; therefore, girls do not often picture themselves in sports or in sports careers. Ten-year-old Susan complains that when she goes to the neighborhood park to play baseball with her brother and father, other boys who have formed a team won't let her join them. They automatically reject her because she is a girl.

Yet participating in sports is one of the best things for a girl to do. Studies have shown that girl athletes tend to do better in school and have more self-esteem. They are more likely to stay away from drugs, score well on achievement tests, and stay in school. Indeed, despite her injuries, Cheryl did extremely well in volleyball and in her senior year of high school was offered a full scholarship to Harvard.

Think about your own upbringing. Were you encouraged to be physically active, or was your family's emphasis on girls looking pretty, being passive, and cheering the boys on? How do you think your athletic or other physical activity (or lack of it) as a girl influenced you as an adolescent? How did it influence your body image, self-esteem, and peer relationships with both boys and other girls? How did it influence you as an adult? Are you physically active now? How do you feel about your daughter being on a soccer or a baseball team?

You can encourage the girl in your life by starting her in sports at an early age. The most important factor in girls learning to enjoy their bodies through movement is parental encouragement. It is helpful if you are modeling some form of physical activity yourself; it doesn't have to be competitive. Whether you're walking, bicycling, or working out at a gym, show her that you value your own physical well-being.

If you or your husband are not good role models in this regard, because of illness or lack of interest or time, try to find a mentor for your daughter who is involved with sports or other physical activity. An aunt or coach at school can initiate, guide, and encourage her to do her best. Introduce her to female athletes through articles, books, or videos. A good role model shows girls what is possible—females can participate in sports and succeed. The role model can be a professional basketball player, a sports writer, or your next-door neighbor who walks every day.

Even if you are not a sports fan or physically skilled yourself, you can model values that will help your daughter in doing sports. Teach her to ride a bicycle as soon as she is old enough. Take her to a local park, where she can run and play on the monkey bars, swings, and slides. These activities help her develop strength, balance, and coordination. Nature walks or hikes will also challenge her physically, and she will gain confidence in her body. If she asks you to throw a baseball or kick a soccer ball or do a cartwheel, give it a try in order to show her that you are willing to risk failing or looking silly. This is an important attitude to have when playing sports.

Stacey started swimming regularly when she was pregnant with her third child. Now she swims outdoors every day in a heated pool and likes relating to the seasonal changes that way. She finds her swim laps meditative and restorative: "I can go in any emotional state—tired, anxious, or excited—and leave feeling grounded. I also like the nice feeling, the easy exchanges with other women in the locker room; no one has a role." For a while, Stacey swam in meets, and her school-age daughters, Sarah and Becky, came to watch her compete. The girls were accustomed to their mother attending their games and meets, which made Stacey's competition a fun role reversal for all of them. Her girls have developed physical activities of their own. Sarah now has a Pilates studio, where she teaches people with injuries to regain their physical strength and health; Becky prefers to be outdoors and likes to hike and camp.

Positive role models in books for girls also show them that physical activity is possible in their own lives. Good books for encouraging girls to do sports convey the message that having fun is the main reason to participate. For older girls, books that include the complexity of their preteen changing identities are helpful.

Cat Running by Zilpha Keatley Snyder is an excellent book, set during the Great Depression of the 1930s, about Catherine, who is the fastest runner in her school. But her old-fashioned, stingy father won't let her wear slacks in the sixth-grade girls' race even though all the other girls wear them. Cat is so mad that she decides not to race at all, and a barefooted "Okie" from the camp near Cat's home wins the race. Cat befriends his little sister and encounters poverty and prejudice. At the story's end, Cat's running becomes a matter of life and death for the little girl, and a journey of self-discovery for Cat. The book ends with Cat as a heroine, reconciled with her father.

It is important to encourage a girl to do a sport or physical activity to which she is naturally drawn from her own experience. If she enjoys her sport, she will stick with it. As a parent, it is best to let your daughter watch and try a variety of activities so that she has a good range of choices. But many parents make the mistake of choosing for their daughters, or they unconsciously expect their daughters to do what they wished they had done as children. If a girl is motivated in a particular direction, a parent's encouragement and upholding the value of discipline (for example, adhering to an often demanding practice schedule) ensures her continued interest. Be attentive to your daughter's likes and dislikes as she develops and give her as many choices as possible. Remember that some girls prefer the rough-and-tumble of group sports whereas others like individual activities. Be sure to expose the girl in your life to both.

Teamwork, Team Sports

In team sports, a girl learns how to work toward a goal with others. She learns rules that she has to abide by for the sake of group performance. And she learns to sometimes forgo her individual feelings or wishes for the good of the whole. Baseball, soccer, basketball, and volleyball all require cooperation, determination, and endurance. Self-esteem is one of the factors that will influence her desire to play one of these sports.

Another influential factor is *self-efficacy*, a term coined by social psychologist Albert Bandura to refer to a situation-specific self-confidence that indicates the strength and level at which one believes one can successfully perform a skill. In other words, self-efficacy is a girl's judgment of her ability to use the skills she possesses—her confidence, her belief in her strength and capability. The implication is that even if a girl has the strength and the skill to do something, if she doesn't believe that she can do it, she will not choose to participate.

Therefore, a sense of self-efficacy can influence a girl's choice of activity, the amount of effort she puts into it, and her willingness to persist in an activity even in the face of failure. Therefore, it influences her performance, both present and future. Studies found that the four main sources of a sense of self-efficacy are a previous record of failure or success in the activity; vicarious experiences; verbal persuasion by coaches, mentors, or parents; and self-interest.

The two areas in which most of the research on self-efficacy has been done thus far are sports and mathematics. The studies showed that a girl's sense of self-efficacy increased when she thought math or a sport was useful, saw the task as gender-appropriate, and had had past experience with it. Because both math and basketball have traditionally been identified as male areas of activity—most of the people that a girl has seen succeeding in these activities will have been male—girls have low self-efficacy in those areas. Making sure that your daughter has female role models—even videotapes of girls or women performing successfully in sports—will help go against this stereotype.

Girls with high self-efficacy expectations in a given skill are more successful in performing it. Lia took gymnastics for two years, from age four to six. She stopped when her schedule became too full with other extracurricular activities. Then, when Lia was nine, she caught a glimpse of a gymnastics competition on television during the Summer Olympics. She was so captivated that her father taped the event, which often aired after her bedtime, for her to watch the next day. She became fascinated with the girls' performances and watched the tape over and over again that Summer, insisting that she wanted to resume her lessons.

When she returned in the fall, her coach was amazed at her proficiency. Her vicarious experience of watching the Olympic competitors had inspired Lia and taught her some difficult moves. And she had had some preliminary motor experience in those early two years of being successful at it; her self-efficacy for gymnastics was very high. She is dedicated to gymnastics to this day, going twice a week because she loves it so much.

Lia's love of gymnastics has required commitment on my part, because the closest gym is a half hour away in rush-hour traffic, but seeing her deep emotional and physical well-being has superseded the drawbacks.

Trust your daughter's preoccupations and fantasies. You never can tell where girlhood passions will lead. Ann Bancroft, the first woman to travel across the North and South Poles, said that she began having dreams about cold faraway places in junior high school. She was not a good student and preferred to sleep outside in the backyard with her dog most nights. Her mother let her do this, and Ann feels that this was one of the best things her mother did for her. Later, Ann led an all-women team across the Antarctic, each member pulling a two-hundred-pound sled.

Moving Body, Moving Mind

Organized sports are not the only form of healthy physical activity that you can encourage your daughter to do. Any activity in which she uses her body, including singing, acting, dancing, or playing an instrument, engages her physically and mentally. Mental and physical activity strengthen one another; the brain functions better in a healthy body.

Daria began doing Irish step-dancing when she was seven and showed signs of being a natural performer. This dancing has required commitment and discipline on the part of both Rose and Daria. For the past seven years, Rose has supervised her practice in their living room. She watches and gives Daria feedback about her posture and steps. When Daria wants to practice alone, her mother leaves the room. At times, Rose has arranged for Daria to visit a friend's exercise studio so her daughter will have the benefit of seeing herself reflected in wall-to-wall mirrors.

Rose is committed to supporting her daughter's practice and participation in competitions, because she sees that it enhances Daria's strength and self-confidence. Grace, concentration, memory, and timing are necessary for the difficult sequence of dance steps; it is also a great aerobic exercise. Rose loves watching her daughter perform, because she herself has always loved music. And Rose did not have the opportunity to excel physically when she was a girl. As an adult, she has taken up a daily half-hour exercise program on a Nordic Track machine, because she has seen the benefit of dance to her daughter.

Daria chose her Irish step-dancing costume for wearing in competitions. Her short black velvet dress with an Irish lace collar is lined in purple satin and embroidered on the skirt, bodice, and sleeves with a design from the Book of Kells, and it has rhinestones splashed all over it. With a matching black velvet cape, her hair curled in bouncy ringlets, and her strong body, Daria is a fairy-tale picture of the champion Irish step-dancer that she is. She and her mother and father are proud of her, and Rose has renewed her own energy through participating and encouraging her daughter in her healthy physical development.

The Thrill of Individual Sports

Team sports and physical activities of all kinds are alike in that they help girls develop both respect and responsibility—respect for fellow athletes, performers, coaches, and directors and responsibility for their own actions. But in team sports, the results depend on team effort whereas in individual activities, girls can see a direct relationship between their own efforts and the results.

Twelve-year-old Shaina has been riding horses since she was seven. She loves working with the horse that she rides at the stable. "I like paying attention to every move the horse makes and understanding why he is doing it. I like the relationship and knowing that what I do affects him." One of Shaina's special times with her mother, Camille, is the long drive up to the stables each Sunday morning. Shaina likes talking to her mother in the car and having her watch her lessons. As an individual sport, horseback riding requires self-motivation to do your best, becoming the best rider that you can be. Although Shaina likes to ride and train in the ring, she dreams of a day when she can ride bareback in open country or at the beach. Shaina, a confident horsewoman, knows that when that day comes, she will be able to take the opportunity and run with it.

Girls do not always have the same opportunities that boys do in athletic fields. And daily P.E. is often not required just at the age girls need it most—middle school, when their bodies begin to change and self-esteem begins to slip. But by the time a girl reaches middle school, if she has been supported in doing so, she can be involved in extracurricular group sports or individual athletics either in or outside of school, for example, soccer, gymnastics, track, volleyball, or basketball.

Your adolescent will be happier and more balanced if she is

physically active. Studies by psychologist Linda Covey and others on physical activity and adolescent girls' psychological development show that active girls have a more positive self-image and more coping skills at home and at school than inactive girls. The active girls saw themselves as having more masculine and feminine characteristics and, of course, higher physical ability ratings than inactive girls. In teenage girls, physical activity also results in healthier emotional expression and emotional control.

Active girls with a high sense of self-efficacy are often successful in more than one field. Figure skater Kathleen Kelly Cutone dropped out of competition after college, after finishing fourteenth in the nationals. Now, after completing law school and getting married, she is back training and juggling her sport, her marriage, and her law career.

It is important, however, to avoid a cycle of pressure to overachieve. Like many of her friends, Lia's problem is that she is drawn to many activities—drama, singing, gymnastics, basketball, and writing—each of which demands much time and commitment out of school. My job as a mother is often to help her limit her choices, to help her decide what she wants to do most so that she does not become overextended.

Each girl will find the physical activity that suits her if given the freedom and support to explore her inclinations. But be aware that your daughter may encounter obstacles as a young female athlete seeking autonomy in areas traditionally dominated by men.

The girl's cross-country team from Gulliver Preparatory School in Miami placed third in the second-largest division of their state meet. But officials disqualified them from the championship meet in the fall of 1995 because they wore close-fitting nylon and lycra shorts; the Florida officials said they came up too high on the girls' legs. These briefs, designed to promote comfort, free movement, and a feeling of speed are worn regularly by leading high-school girls nationwide who emulate Olympic winners and collegiate role models. Jessica Atrio, the team captain, said, "We felt violated. Cross-country is about your time and place, not what you wear." One of the coaches said, "I've seen girls run in those briefs for years. Officials seem to be more interested in looking at girls' rear ends than their athletic prowess."

If your daughter has such an experience, let her know that you support her, even if you cannot change the rules. Help with the appeals process. Whatever the outcome, your support of her will help build her character to continue fighting for her rights.

Your daughter may be the only girl on her Little League baseball team. Cheer her on. Be an unconditional fan of your girl's games and meets. Get to know her coach so you can assess whether fun and participation are emphasized as well as skills. You will also be able to discuss your opinion of his or her coaching with your daughter after the games.

Teach your daughter to be a good sport, to treat opposing coaches and referees the way she would like to be treated. Always encourage fair play. It's more of a challenge to be a good sport after losing the game than after winning it. Respond to an injured player immediately; stop the game. Root for your child and her team to play well. Do not tolerate abusive or obscene language or taunting by any player or coach or use it yourself. Do not embarrass the officials or your daughter.

Confidence in Her Body

Self-confidence and self-awareness are grounded in a girl's feeling of confidence in her body. The most common psychological problems in girls are deeply bound up with a disturbed body image. Sherry was such a big baby that she was off the growth chart at birth. In 1969, the prevailing medical opinion was "Don't give her too much food—she's too big." All through grammar school, Vi, a young mother, dutifully tried to help Sherry diet. Now Vi wishes she had known to let Sherry's appetite govern how much she ate.

It was always difficult to find anything that would fit the outsize girl. One day when Sherry was in second grade, she and her mother went shopping for clothes. Sherry was crying as they drove home, and her mother pulled to the side of the road to comfort her. Vi put her arms around her daughter and said, "Oh, Sherry, I know it's hard, such a struggle with your body." When Vi began driving again, Sherry wrote a note and tossed it on her mother's lap. The note said, "My Mom is so bold." Vi was touched that her young daughter appreciated that her mother was trying to help her.

Vi feels good that she did encourage and share exercising with Sherry—not to shame her about her body, but to develop and tone it. All through middle school and high school, Vi and Sherry would run together every morning for twenty to twenty-five minutes.

This was so important to Sherry that when Vi gave birth to a baby boy when Sherry was fourteen, Vi would go along on the runs in the car, nursing the baby, just to keep Sherry company. Sherry is now 6′1″ and continues to exercise as an independent, successful woman at age twenty-six.

By supporting her involvement in physical activity, you will enhance your daughter's sense of well-being and pride in her body. Studies by the Melpomene Institute for Women's Health Research and others show that good body image in girls is reliant on positive comments from parents, friends, and peers. Melpomene was said to have been a Greek woman who in 1896 requested entry in the Olympic marathon. The Olympic committee refused, saying that long-distance running was not physiologically suited to women. Melpomene defied them and trained for three weeks to compete with men in the twenty-six-mile trial at a time of four and a half hours. In appreciation of her courage, stamina, and dedication to the athletic life, the Institute for Women's Health Research, which emphasizes physical activity for women of all ages, was named after her.

As a parent, take every opportunity to celebrate your daughter's physical activities. Whether she bicycles, swims, plays basketball, or does gymnastics, ballet, or track, find a way to incorporate her physical activity into the celebrations that you create for her. The emphasis should always be on her involvement, rather than on her winning the race. Attending a team dinner for parents at the end of her basketball season is an important ritual. You may want to add a special surprise of your own when you get home. Or you could plan a dinner after an important gymnastics meet for your daughter. Have each person offer a toast to her athletic skill, regardless of where she placed. Dedicate the dinner to her talent and commitment. Her self-esteem will grow as her endeavors are celebrated, not just her triumphs.

With violence against women and girls higher than it has ever been, it is important to teach our daughters to defend themselves. To protect them from being preyed upon in this society, girls must have self-concepts that include strength. Girls want their strengths to be acknowledged and valued. Diedre, an eleven year old, expresses frustration about being cast in a weaker role than her brother. "Why do adults praise me for being nice and cute and my brother for being brave and strong? I'm brave and strong too! And I'm going to prove it!"

Polly, who has taught middle school for fifteen years, has three girls under age twelve. She jokingly referred to her child-rearing practices as the "risk method." She favored her daughters' playing outside, making forts, and letting them run around the neighborhood without shirts until her oldest was ten years old. Their favorite game was playing "wild circus children." Polly said she wanted to encourage adventuresome characters in her girls.

Many self-defense programs for girls are now offered through middle and high schools that focus on necessary skills at different ages. But your girl's awareness of her own strength, her ability to assert herself, to say "NO," and, if necessary, to defend herself, is first established in her home environment. Protecting her physical and emotional safety from birth, giving her useful information at each stage of her upbringing, as well as showing respect for her developing autonomy are all helpful. But you must also celebrate her strength, encouraging skills that make her independent and self-reliant. Although karate or judo specifically train her to defend herself, any sport will enhance her self-esteem and strengthen her ability to take care of herself and stand up for what she believes in.

Trying new things helps a girl challenge herself and become confident in her identity, instead of succumbing to wanting to be in the "in group." Encourage her to try a new sport just to experiment with how it feels. Emphasize participating and doing her best. Making new choices available to her, particularly at times when she is having social difficulties, is a healthy, usually successful way to help her feel better about herself.

There are many destructive options for middle-school and high-school girls—experimentation with drugs, alcohol, and promiscuous sexuality, to name three; therefore, it is good to be aware of your girl's state of mind and body. Be sensitive and offer healthy, positive options that are immediately accessible.

If she is feeling isolated and friendless, find out what team sports are currently being offered at her school and talk to her about going out for one of them. Keep in mind that studies have shown that same-sex sports increase self-efficacy in girls, whereas on all-boys' school teams, boy's self-efficacy/confidence decreased. On an all-girl team, she may both boost her self-confidence and make new friends. Or help her audition for the next drama production.

If the school does not offer much in the way of extracurricular activities, think about her inclinations and talents and find an outside place where she can explore one of them. Even teenagers respond to such parental interest in their well-being.

If you work long hours and your girls have a lot of unsupervised free time in the Summer, look into athletic activities at the local Parks and Recreation Department. These facilities offer a wide range of inexpensive programs that your daughter or granddaughter can profit from, including basketball, gymnastics, acting, and volleyball. Find a program that suits the age of each of your children, and you can go to work knowing that they are spending a good chunk of their time doing something that is building their positive body image and general self-esteem.

Active Initiation at Puberty

For her first menstruation or coming-of-age ceremony, your daughter is the center of attention—the star—by virtue of her inner initiation. This moment is hers. She is to be one-in-herself for this event. Her body is changing from within. Having her first blood means that she is a strong and healthy girl. In all puberty ceremonies, in addition to the attention paid to dress and touch, there are also active elements. The running and corn grinding that the Navajo girl does emphasize and enhance her endurance and her strength. These activities bring out her vitality. They are part of her active beauty.

In Janet's Navajo ceremony, her father drove her out into the desert on the third day to tie a ribbon around a pine tree, chosen for being approximately her height; this tree marked the distance that she would run on the fourth day. He told her in a gentle tone, "The longer you run, the longer you can endure life without suffering. You run with the idea that you will not tire out, that you will have strength." The rigorous demands of running and corn grinding bring an added dimension to the adorning and massaging. With these physical challenges, she transforms herself.

For our daughters, the equivalent elements are drawn from their personal realm of physical activities. In a private ritual, if your daughter loves to play soccer, she could kick the ball at a specific point in her coming-of-age ceremony, or a soccer ball could be included on her altar. This will honor her strength and avoid any confusion for her that "soccer isn't feminine." If she is an enthusiastic gymnast, she could turn cartwheels or do back flips.

During this time, you can encourage and support your daughter in using her body in a healthy way. A prepubescent girl needs to be gently taught to protect her sensitive budding breasts at the same time as she is supported to participate fully in active sports like tennis or volleyball.

Preteen girls in the classroom become more self-conscious, more shy than boys. Girls are reluctant to raise their hands and speak up, because their changing bodies make them uncomfortable with people looking at them. This adds to middle-school girls' difficulty both academically and socially. Other factors, such as a girl's verbal self-confidence, self-assertion skills, and previous academic performance, also influence her participation in class. But Polly, who teaches history and social studies, says that what seems to counteract this tendency is that girls who are physically active "have physical bravado" and are more comfortable projecting themselves in the classroom.

When a girl's body begins to change, she may have to make some adjustments in her sports schedule. Knowing about her menstrual cycle and the emotional and psychological ramifications of her cyclical inner life will help a girl access her strength and make the most of her sports.

When a girl begins menstruating, she may have new feelings of needing a day off from school or basketball practice. Where previously she was always ready to play, now she may want to be alone, to read or write or draw in her journal. Validate these feelings in her. In many Native American, African, and South American cultures, a girl is secluded during and after her first period. During her seclusion, she is taught the art of womanhood by older women of the community. Some tribes have ritual seclusion once a month for menstruating women and girls. This gives the women an opportunity to move away from the usual demands of family and community and to take care of their own needs.

From a modern girl's perspective, the need for time alone arises psychologically—it is a need for cyclical introversion. If she pays attention to this new need, she will find herself refreshed and renewed to return to her normal sports, school, and social activities. Encourage your daughter to take this time for reflection. As she grows older, she will find that this time deepens in importance for her psychological and physical health.

But be sensitive to the individual girl in your life; follow her lead. If she wants to play in her baseball game when she is menstruating, that is fine. The point is for her to learn to pay attention to her inner rhythms; it will take time and experimenting with how she feels for her to know herself in this way.

Jana remembers with regret that when she was in public high school, girls were socially ostracized if they did not do P.E. when they were menstruating. "The message was: *Be extroverted, pretend it isn't happening, be stalwart like a soldier, and dress for P.E.*" When roll was called, each girl who had her period raised her hand and said, "First day, regular participating." This announced to the class that she was stoic and brave. "If you bowed out of P.E., you were a wimp, a wuss, a cry-baby." Jana is sad that the message she and other girls internalized was: *Transcend your body. Don't give in;* instead of, *Listen to your body and value what it is saying to you.* Like other women, Jana has spent many years undoing the damage of cultural lessons that went against her feminine nature.

Teach your daughter the details of her fertility cycle, the appearance of fertile flow at ovulation and the hormonal changes leading to blood at menstruation. Explain healthy nutrition, her need for rest, and nonintrusive ways to alleviate cramping as she has her first periods. Discuss the practical options of pads and tampons, plastic or paper or cloth, together with the environmental and physical pros and cons of each choice.

For an older girl, it is helpful to include the special needs of women around their menstrual cycle in this feminine instruction. For example, some girls experience a craving for sweets and a need for more calories in the premenstrual time. Warn your older girls that caffeine and alcohol exacerbate premenstrual and period discomfort; this will help deter them from beginning addictive patterns. Increased carbohydrates and decreased protein intake is recommended for girls and women premenstrually; this helps lessen drastic mood swings in the premenstrual time. Other foods are especially nurturing for a menstruating girl.

If she knows that fried foods, pastries, and candy are going to make her more uncomfortable and grouchy premenstrually, she can choose to avoid those foods. This is positive nutritional self-control. Choosing fruits, vegetables, and whole-grain breads at that time of the month becomes self-nurturance, not self-deprivation. Knowledge of her own body is power. The more she knows, the more informed choices she has, the stronger she will be and the less likely she will be to ignore her body's signals for what she needs.

By educating a girl in this way, the importance of food as energy is communicated. Listening to her body's wisdom about what to eat, and when, empowers a girl to nurture herself instead of obsessing about her weight. An obsession with weight results in a self-destructive preoccupation with negative "self-control," which means that a girl tries to control feelings or desires arising spontaneously within her that do not fit the restrictive cultural norms of how women should look and act.

If your daughter or the girl in your life is too shy, embarrassed, or defensive to discuss these issues with you, make the information available in book or pamphlet form so that she has access to it when she is alone. Letting her know that you value self-care for yourself and for her, and that you find the specific information helpful, is more important than reading the pamphlet or book together. But, if your usual rapport with her is based on that kind of intimacy, sharing the learning also deepens your relationship.

Participating in sports fosters her body awareness. Help her experiment with gentle activity, such as doing a series of yoga postures, swimming, or an easy walk, which can sometimes help ease the pain of cramping. A girl who plays sports or dances easily tunes in to her body and her menstruation. An active girl has a better chance of relating to her menstruation in a healthy way to create a lifelong pattern of well-being.

TEN

Walking into Beauty: Coming of Age and Sexuality

ALL ALONG THE WAY in a girl's development, she needs to be listened to and talked to by the important women in her life. In school, she will be taught a lot about the objective world and its important knowledge. If she is interested in math and science, support her and find role models for her in those fields. But no school is going to teach her about the feminine mysteries embedded in her own body. And that knowledge is power, power for her to be and interact in the world, in her chosen fields. She needs to know and be encouraged in her self-care, her chosen activities, and then eventually educated about sexuality. She will gain strength of mind and strength of body.

If her watery origins have been affirmed, her emotions listened to and validated, she will have emotional authenticity and integrity. She will be accepting of all feelings, not just the socially acceptable ones. If she has been shown affection, she will have the ability to tolerate frustration without becoming overwhelmed. She will have the capacity to cope with stress and crisis.

If she has been held and her body has been blessed, she will have physical self-confidence. She will know and be able to assert appropriate boundaries with herself and others. She will have a healthy relationship to food and a good body image and, therefore, a positive self-image.

Through the simple rituals of combing and washing her hair, if we have valued her thoughts and her thinking, she will have a strong mind. She will be capable of flexible thinking and she will know her own mind and trust her own judgment, both intuitive and rational, subjective and objective.

Through attention to her dressing, she will have evolved socially, as an individual, in relation to her peers, to her family, and to the culture. She will be able to be true to herself and to work and play collaboratively with others. She will have learned to distinguish between the values of pop culture and the enduring values of relationship and responsibility, and she will find social meaning in the world.

When she is adorned with jewelry or makeup and she forms

a meaningful relationship to these feminine adornments, she will also develop a sense of her body being a precious container for new life. Her creativity will find expression in all her endeavors. And whether she relates to the spirit in nature, feels reverence for her family's religious beliefs, or goes on a quest for her own spirituality, she will know spiritual well-being.

Through storytelling, a girl will learn about her personal history within the larger history of women. She will have a feminine lineage in which to view herself. She will be able to see her unique gifts in relation to mothers and grandmothers and great-grandmothers and women throughout the centuries who were effective in defining their own lives. She will feel she has a place in the world.

Through strengthening her body in sports or other physical activities, she will be healthy. She will know that she has the capacity to produce change. She will have authority and, if the need arises, she will be able to defend herself in confrontation. She will feel competent and aware.

Secure in her relationship with her mother, confident in her chosen activities, a prepubescent girl raised in this way is infused with self-esteem. She has experienced the greatest gift that she can have as a girl: her mother sharing herself and her wisdom with her daughter. A girl nurtured in this way becomes more outspoken, more defined, more exuberant in her preteen years. Although her ideas and her emotions may fluctuate wildly, she is not afraid to express the extremes. She does not withdraw and begin playing a role. She opens to a beginning of mastering her own capabilities, talents, and goals. With appropriate guidance, she will enter adolescence empowered.

After years of experience doing psychotherapy with women and girls, I have come to see that first menstruation—and the prepubescent years that come before it—is a critical emotional and psychological passage for our daughters toward the women they will become. Once her blood appears, there is no possibility of a girl ignoring or avoiding moving toward womanhood. The time around first menstruation lays down patterns for a girl's subsequent life changes: defloration, sexual identity, fertility, conception, pregnancy, birth, nursing, mothering, and menopause.

The definitive moment of change—the appearance of menstrual blood—that marks the transformation from girl to adolescent is still celebrated in many cultures today. Girls need ceremony, because the physical initiatory experiences that originate in their bodies require that a girl sacrifice her previous physiological state of being and therefore her previous psychological identity. When a girl begins to bleed, she has to start taking care of herself physically in a different way and assume new responsibility for herself emotionally.

The White Mountain Apache acknowledge the interconnection between first puberty and the succeeding passages in a woman's life. In her puberty ceremony, the girl dances with a staff, made especially for her on this occasion. The cane is made of willow, is painted yellow, decorated with small round bells, eagle feathers, a piece of turquoise, and ribbon streamers. As the girl dances, she pounds the cane on the ground, making the bells jingle and the ribbons flutter. Dancing, she listens to the chanting of songs and prayers, which wish her a long life. The cane represents old age; as an old woman, she will use it to help her walk. The abalone shell on her forehead associates her with the power of White Shell Woman or Changing Woman.

The reactions of the people close to a girl as she approaches her first period, is carried in her psyche. Whether we celebrate or denigrate her determines the next several years of her life—her adolescent identity. These same circumstances subtly influence all succeeding physical, emotional, and psychological passages for the rest of her life. If she is joyously celebrated, she moves into adolescence self-confident and proud of herself as a budding woman. If she is made to feel ashamed of her body, she feels tainted with shame and self-loathing for being female.

A girl is often fearful or confused about the change that is gradually arising from inside, affecting her body, emotions, and mind. There is nothing she can do about it; it is like nothing she has experienced before. As she wonders about the day of her first period, she feels reluctant, hesitant, awed. She becomes more vulnerable, which makes her emotionally, physically, and spiritually open to change. If the women around her respond sensitively and lovingly at this time, she will be able to gradually embrace the change.

In planned celebrations, including other women and girl-friends provides a sense of community—an ever-widening circle of sharing feminine wisdom. Some families include fathers and brothers in supporting roles. One young girl chose to select different people from among her family and friends to talk to her about different aspects of her initiation—menstrual wisdom, sexuality, pregnancy, the male perspective on women. She had a dinner with each of them, and then all of them were invited to a party in her honor.

In most traditional girls' puberty ceremonies, as in the Lese tribe, where men make the cloth for the girl's dress, fathers often participate in a meaningful, though secondary, way. In the Jewish Bat Mitzvah, performed for girls at age thirteen or fourteen, the father has an important role during the girl's preparation and in the ceremony itself. Both father and mother present their daughter with a prayer shawl in the ritual. The father also does a special blessing before and after she reads her Torah portion.

In my son's peer group, three girls had Bat Mitzvahs to which the whole eighth-grade class was invited. As her classmates, family, and friends watched, each girl stood on the altar, read her portion of the Sacred Scroll, and was acknowledged in an elaborate ceremony. Later, her classmates ate festive meals and danced joyfully into the night. All the boys and girls present were able to vicariously experience their initiatory stage of life.

In Janet's Navajo ceremony in 1986, a medicine man officiated and Janet's father, a lawyer, helped at various times over the course of the four-day ritual. On the first day, he pointed out the direction of her dawn run and showed her how to mark the spot where she stopped by tying a ribbon to a shrub. He took a turn stirring her cake batter when she got tired. Later, he robed her with a Pendleton shawl before she blessed the ceremonial cake with corn pollen. Most impressive, he was an attentive presence throughout the ceremony, offering strong support for his daughter's coming of age. He said to Janet, "Entering the role of womanhood, in the Navajo way, you give gifts to the people. Everything you touch is blessed with your womanhood."

For our daughters, the inclusion of fathers and brothers must come out of our family dialogue, with utmost respect for the girl's wishes. Include the important men in your daughter's life in whatever way seems appropriate to her and to you. A father's role will emerge from the unique relationship that he has had with his daughter. Rebekah spent the night in the forest by herself the night before her puberty ceremony. Her father slept in a sleeping bag near her small shelter, at some distance but close enough to be called if she sensed any danger.

Sleeping alone on a dark mountain was a challenge for Rebekah that symbolized her entry into another stage of life. After returning home the next day, she was bathed and dressed by her mother and other close women friends before the ceremony. Then Rebekah's father walked her to the ceremony while her younger brother scattered rose petals before her. Her mother walked behind them in this procession. Twenty-five women and girls, aged ten to sixty, were waiting to celebrate her, Lia and I among them. At the door, her father and brother kissed her good-bye.

Inside, Rebekah entered the circle we had formed and was presented to the group by her mother. We had each been asked to bring a bead as a gift. As each woman threaded her bead on a thin red cord, she spoke to Rebekah, offering good wishes, telling little stories, or passing on hard-earned wisdom. Several women spoke of their own sadness at not having had an honoring of their body and their blood when they were young. The young girls who had begun to bleed and had had ceremonies themselves had a lot of positive experience to offer. The youngest girls, the uninitiated, chose to remain silent as they strung their beads. The making of the necklace took a long time; it was very satisfying and astonishingly beautiful. Later, after a ceremony in which the necklace was placed around Rebekah's neck, we had a delicious feast.

In some cases, a simple one-to-one acknowledgment is more appropriate. A mother often likes to take her daughter out for a nice intimate dinner after her first menstruation. Do what feels comfortable to you, and it will be wonderful and special. For a puberty ceremony, you and your daughter can begin planning in advance as she acknowledges the early signs of her body changing. Or you can do something impromptu together on the day she begins bleeding. Or, when she bleeds for the first time, you can start to plan a ceremony to take place within the year.

If your daughter is too modest to share much of her changing experience at puberty with you, celebrate her femininity indirectly by giving her a gift that she can use by herself, for instance a luxurious bath oil, a pretty new journal, or a book that you enjoyed when you were her age. Without discussion, these kinds of gestures acknowledge your appreciation of her young womanhood.

A girl raised in a positive mother-daughter relationship and celebrated from birth is wonderfully prepared to create and enjoy a powerful ceremony around the time of her first period. But a mother's wish to honor her with a positive rite of passage often meets with resistance from the pubescent daughter, especially if ceremony has not been part of her upbringing in younger years. There are ways, however, that you can seize the moment and honor your daughter's first blood. Stacey, for example, knowing her daughter Becky's temperament, simply called her out on the deck one evening when they were preparing dinner together and gave her an apple to fling as far as she could in honor of her first bleeding.

Creating Ceremonies

Marking transitions in a girl's life helps to alleviate the trepidation that she is feeling about her changing. Even if she cannot respond to your positive gesture out of embarrassment or moodiness, it will help her sense of herself. No matter how difficult her temperament, at age six or sixteen, a girl will feel loved and appreciated if she finds a tiny wrapped gift or nice note on her pillow or bedside table when she awakes the next morning, after surviving a difficult first day at school or after mastering a challenging task. And such gestures will keep the relationship door open between you, providing an avenue for her to come to you when she needs you.

Be creative. You and your daughter can have fun finding or writing your own stories, poems, dreams, and myths. Collaborating on celebrations strengthens your bond. Many arts—drawing, painting, sewing, music, drama, and dance—play a central part in puberty rituals. In the Navajo girl's ceremony, the girl is transformed into a woman through songs; your daughter could sing a favorite song or choose a song for the group to sing. In certain African tribes, special designs are drawn or tattooed on a girl's body when her period begins, designs that are then elaborated at other significant moments in her life, for example, after the birth of her first child. Having her ears pierced or her face painted might appeal to your daughter. In the White Mountain Apache tribe, the white buckskin dress is sewn for the girl to wear in her ceremony; shopping for a special dress or letting your daughter borrow a dress of yours that she has admired are possibilities for a modern girl's ceremony. In the Tukuna Amazon tribe, the honored girl must perform a ritual swim in the river. Your daughter could go to her favorite place in nature for a ritual swim. Engaging your daughter and her individual talents and achievements in designing rituals for her passages will bring her into her femininity in a creative way.

Rose took Daria to a group initiation ceremony at the Menstrual Health Foundation: Coming of Age Project in Sebastopol, California. Five mothers and their preteen daughters who had recently had their first periods participated in a day-long program. After a brief introduction by coordinator Tamara Slayton, the mothers adjourned to talk among themselves about their own experiences of puberty and menstruation. The girls were shown slides and given a two-hour instruction by Tamara on their fertility cycles. They discussed how to chart their menstruation and their options for using commercial pads, tampons, or natural-fiber menstrual cloths. The girls drew pictures of their wombs and fallopian tubes and had an opportunity to ask questions.

When their mothers rejoined them, they each made a doll. The instructions were: "Make a doll that expresses how you see yourself." Many emotions surfaced during the process: The girls struggled to deal with the changes their bodies were going through as they fashioned their dolls' bodies; their mothers struggled with their body images as adults. During the making of the dolls, Rose saw Daria relax and become absorbed in herself and her creativity. Next, the women and girls made crowns of gold foil, dried flowers, ribbon, and lace. Later, the fathers arrived bearing gifts, a large cake was presented, and the mothers ceremonially crowned their daughters, each saying something about what she wanted for her daughter as she matured.

The age at which your daughter has her first period determines how much or whether sexuality is explored as part of this education. With younger girls (ages nine to eleven), the focus of what is presented needs to remain on their own bodies and how to take care of themselves during their periods, with a positive feeling about themselves and their bleeding. Such a ceremony with its careful preparation clears the way for frank, increasingly complex discussions about sexuality at each stage of your girl becoming sexual.

Depending on a girl's emotional maturity and age (especially age thirteen to fifteen), it may be appropriate to include discussion about sexuality in her coming-of-age ceremony. If your daughter is reluctant to discuss sexuality at all, try to create ongoing opportunities for her to make a confidante of a trusted relative or friend.

It is important to share your values about sexuality with your older daughter. Talk to her about the difference between sexuality for pleasure and intimacy, and sexuality for having a child. Bring up the importance of her choosing her first sexual experience so that it will be a positive one. As Karen Bouris says in her book *The First Time: What Parents and Teenage Girls Should Know About*

"Losing Your Virginity," "It is possible to pass on a better legacy to our daughters than either the repressed attitudes of the fifties or the promiscuous ones of the sixties and seventies."

Talk to your daughter about some of the situations that she may face with peers that will make sex an unpleasant or dangerous situation; for example, abusing alcohol and other drugs, being in an unsafe place, being with someone she barely knows, or giving in to a boy's pressure to have sexual contact. Discuss having sex without intercourse (kissing, sensations of arousal, orgasm) and her choice of contraception. And try to prepare her for the emotional involvement that inevitably comes with having a sexual life. Talk about her choosing the right time for herself and about choosing a sensitive partner, one who is willing to talk about feelings. Remember, an adolescent girl who does not understand who she is, and is unable to assert herself in her relationships, will focus on boys' needs and pleasure.

Sex education in schools emphasizes biology and diseases such as AIDS but does not include the psychological or emotional aspects of sexuality. In a puberty ceremony, the crucial factor is that all education be appropriately given to the girl, imparted in the context of her "walking into beauty," becoming an adolescent girl.

Storytelling is a helpful way to share this kind of information. Creating an atmosphere that is based on trust and love where emotions can be expressed is essential. Humor also has a role in such intimate conversations. Jana remembers that one of the ways she and her daughter Kate broke the ice to talk about sex was that thirteen-year-old Kate was worried about her promiscuous sixteen-year-old stepsister, Carol, who lived with their dad. Carol (who couldn't talk to her own mother) would talk to Kate about her bad choice of boys, and Kate would talk to her mother. Jana had an opportunity to voice her values about sexual relationship and give advice about contraception. "Kate trusted me enough to come to me, and those conversations paved the way for intimate talks with Kate later about her sexuality." Do not hesitate to share your sexual values with your daughters. Not talking about sex increases the risk that it will happen in an unhealthy or unsafe way.

Rites of Passage

Rites of passage can take many different forms, some simple, some elaborate. Various ones are suggested in this book. You may create your own in a step-by-step way, or you may find yourself spontaneously initiating informal rituals with your daughter. As your relationship with her develops, intimate conversations can take on a ritual connotation. You can plan larger rituals for your daughter by choosing an element from one chapter of this book or by combining the elements in several chapters for more elaborate ceremonies. As you look through the chapters, you will naturally improvise or interject elements that are personally meaningful to your daughter or to your family.

A pubescent girl may draw pictures or write poetry for the text of her coming-of-age ceremony; or she may wish to write and enact a drama by herself or with others to celebrate her transformation and new status. Girls approaching puberty often have powerful dreams about their first menstruation. They dream of being celebrated, singled out, or shown special magic, or they see visions of their future at this time. Ask your daughter or granddaughter about her dreams; encourage her to write them down. You may see images in them that will help you plan a celebration for her. And when she is twenty, thirty, or forty years old and has lived into the dreams, she will be able to reread them and marvel at what her psyche already knew. Encourage her to use her dreams in this way.

Understanding herself as female gives a girl solid inner ground. Such self-awareness and confidence prepares her for a healthy, productive life as an adult woman, whether she chooses to be a mother, an artist, a businesswoman, or all three. And when she encounters male bias in our culture, she will have the healthy self-esteem to see the inequality and stand up for herself.

The Creative Adolescent Girl

When a girl is raised with an attitude of valuing the feminine, valuing who she is, she moves naturally toward a positive, meaningful experience of menstruation. Her mother and other significant women in her life have told her what she needs to know about her changing body in an age-appropriate ongoing conversation. Her sense of connection, of being cared about by adult women, has given her psychological resilience. She knows that she is different from boys and has been taught the difficulties of being a woman in a patriarchal culture. If she has not had an optimal experience of herself as a girl child, her preteen years provide an opportunity to reorient her to her own blossoming femininity as a source of joy and pride.

Recently, I spoke to a conference on girls' puberty ceremonies and their psychological value for modern women. During the question-and-answer period, a woman in her fifties, expressed her sadness at not having given her thirty-year-old daughter an understanding and valuing of her femininity. This older mother felt the sadness both for her daughter and for herself. She said, however, that now that her daughter had borne a girl child of her own, the alienation between herself and her adult daughter was beginning to dissolve. The mother said that she felt, after seeing the slides of the Navajo girl's ceremony, that she could further heal something with her daughter by honoring her granddaughter in special feminine ways. Perhaps, she mused, there was also a way to celebrate or ritualize a new stage in her relationship with her daughter.

Most women in our culture feel the sadness, the loss of not being raised with meaningful feminine guidance or values. Recognizing those feelings of sadness and loss can lead you to a new positive appreciation and celebration of your own femininity, or to a renewed relationship with your daughter, mother, or another girl in your life. A study of Wellesley students found that college girls continued to express a desire for increased connection with their mothers. They anticipated more contact with them, hoping that their own well-being and changes as young adults might contribute to their mothers' development. Girls expected an even more intense relationship as they grew older and became mothers themselves.

If your early-adolescent daughter is withdrawing from you, take her on a retreat, just the two of you. Choose a place she likes—the beach, hot springs, the mountains, or a favorite people-watching spot in the city—to get her out of her usual environment. With time to relax together and to listen to her, you may find out what is troubling her, what pressures she is experiencing at school and in her social life.

Elaine has found long drives with fourteen-year-old Jenevieve to be the perfect way to unwind from the family routine. They listen to Jenevieve's music in the car, stop at a beachside cafe to eat, spend the night at a bed-and-breakfast, then explore the beach together the next day. Collecting shells, wading in the surf, and letting the sound of the waves fill them, they find their connection again. With time to be together, to listen to one another, you may find your way back to an earlier intimacy with your daughter that surrounded the daily rituals of holding, bathing, and haircombing. You may also find a new intellectual rapport.

If you are the mother of an adult daughter and wish that you had been more developed as a woman when you raised her, you may find ways to talk to her about what you wished you had done differently. Such conversations between mothers and daughters in adulthood can be miraculously healing. New relationships develop out of self-reflection shared with a grown daughter, at any age. You may find that it is possible for the two of you to create a private celebration that honors your new closeness as you engage in conversation about what you were thinking and feeling as you were raising her. Your openness will also influence your adult daughter with her own daughters. And as a grandmother, you can celebrate your granddaughters in ways that were not possible for you as a young mother in another era.

It is never too late to celebrate and renew feminine values. Whether a girl has a planned ceremony at her first period or an intimate acknowledgment from her mother, the fertile adolescent girl will experience her body being honored, she will be educated about her menstrual cycle, and she will be prepared to begin her young womanhood with her body, soul, and psyche intact. She will feel that she is "walking into beauty" as she approaches womanhood. She will have the capacity to experience menstruation as a time of renewal, ritual withdrawal, and inspiration. And she will have an awareness of her fertility as potential to be used creatively in many ways, not only in bearing children.

In her difficult adolescent years, a girl will always have herself to come back to, her own inner ground, based in her body, in her healthy self-concept. Later on as an adult, she will be strong and capable in making choices that are healthy for her in work and relationships. All that she has gleaned from the women around her, whether she appreciated it at the moment or not, will be synthesized in her individuality as an adult woman. And she will be wonderfully prepared to celebrate the girls—and women—in her own life.

Bibliography
■ ■ ■

Bandura, Albert. *Social Foundations of Thought and Action.* Englewood Cliffs, N.J: Prentice-Hall, 1986.

Belenky, Mary Field, Blythe McVicker Clinchy, Nancy Rule Goldberger, and Jill Mattuck Tarule. *Women's Way of Knowing: The Development of Self, Voice, and Mind.* New York: Basic Books, 1986.

Bouris, Karen. *The First Time: What Parents and Teenage Girls Should Know About "Losing Your Virginity."* Berkeley: Conari Press, 1993, pp. 184–185.

Bradley, Marion Zimmer. *The Mists of Avalon.* New York: Alfred A. Knopf, 1982.

Brown, Lyn Mikel, and Carol Gilligan. *Meeting at the Crossroads: Women's Psychology and Girls' Development.* New York: Ballantine, 1992.

Covey, Linda A. and Deborah L. Feltz. "Physical Activity and Adolescent Female Psychological Development." *Journal of Youth and Adolescence,* vol. 20, no. 4 (August 1991): pp. 463-474.

"Female Smokers Rivaling Men." *San Francisco Chronicle,* 11 July 1994.

"A Figure Skater with a Law Degree." *New York Times,* 17 January 1996.

Ferrero, Pat, Elaine Hedges, and Julie Silber. *Hearts and Hands: The Influence of Women and Quilts on American Society.* San Francisco: Quilt Digest Press, 1987, p. 95.

Frisbie, Charlotte. *Kinaaldá: A Study of the Navajo Girl's Puberty Ceremony.* Middletown, CT: Wesleyan University Press, 1967.

Gilligan, Carol. *In a Different Voice: Psychological Theory and Women's Development.* Cambridge, Mass.: Harvard University Press, 1982.

Gilligan, Carol, Annie G. Rogers, and Deborah L. Tolman, eds. *Women, Girls and Psychotherapy: Reframing Resistance.* New York: Haworth Press, 1991.

Girls Ink. Newsletter of Girls Incorporated. 30 East 33rd St., New York, NY, 10016-5394. Tel. (212) 689-3700.

Goleman, Daniel. *New Woman Magazine,* "How To Get a Grip on Anger." December 1995, pp. 103–4, 124.

Goseyun, Anna Early. "Carla's Sunrise," *Native Peoples: The Art and Lifeways,* vol. 4, no. 4 (Summer 1991): pp. 8–16.

Guccioni, Leslie Davis. *Nobody Listens to Me.* New York: Scholastic, 1991.

Heroes: Growing Up Female and Strong. Video. MELPOMENE Institute for Women's Health Research. 1010 University Ave., St. Paul, MN, 55104. Tel. (612) 642-1951.

Johnson, Holiday. *Body/Mind Magazine,* "Boosting Self-Esteem Through Yoga." September/October 1994, p. 22.

Jordan, Judith V., Alexandra G. Kaplan, Jean Baker Miller, Irene P. Stiver, and Janet L. Surrey. *Women's Growth in Connection. Writings from the Stone Center.* New York: Guilford Press, 1991.

Lasky, Kathryn, and Meribah Knight. *Searching for Laura Ingalls: A Reader's Journal.* New York: Macmillan Publishing Co., 1993.

Lincoln, Bruce. *Emerging from the Chrysalis: Studies in Women's Initiations.* Cambridge, Mass.: Harvard University Press, 1981.

Lirgg, Cathy D. "Effects of Same-Sex Versus Coeducational Physical Education on the Self-Perceptions of Middle and High School Students." *Research Quarterly for Exercise and Sport,* vol. 64, no. 3 (September 1993): p. 324.

Miller, M. L. *Dizzy from Fools.* Natick, Mass.: Picture Book Studios USA, 1985.

"Modern Life Suppresses an Ancient Body Rhythm." *New York Times*, 14 March 1995.

"The Navajo Puberty Ceremony." *The Indian Trader: The Western and Indian Arts and Crafts Publication*. P.O. Box 1421, Gallup, NM, October 1986, 18–19.

NEW MOON: *The Magazine for Girls and Their Dreams* and NEW MOON NETWORK: *For Adults Who Care About Girls*. Published by Nancy Gruver and Joe Kelly with an editorial board of girls. P.O. Box 3587, Duluth, MN, 55803-3587. Tel. (218) 728-5507.

Northrup, Christiane, M.D. *Women's Bodies, Women's Wisdom: Creating Physical and Emotional Health and Healing*. New York: Bantam Books, 1994.

Orenstein, Peggy and the American Association of University Woman. *Schoolgirls: Young Women, Self-Esteem and the Confidence Gap*. New York: Doubleday Books, 1994, p. xiv.

Panofsky, Dora, and Erwin Panofsky. *Pandora's Box: The Changing Aspects of a Mythical Symbol*. Bollingen Series LII. Princeton: Princeton University Press, 1956.

Pipher, Mary. *Reviving Ophelia: Saving the Selves of Adolescent Girls*. New York: Ballantine, 1994, p. 291.

Porter, A. P. *Kwanzaa*. Minneapolis: Cavolrhoda Books, 1991.

Pullman, Philip. *The Ruby in the Smoke*. New York: Random House, 1985.

————. *Shadow in the North*. New York: Alfred A. Knopf, 1986.

————. *The Tiger in the Well*. New York: Alfred A. Knopf, 1990.

Quintero, Nita. "Coming of Age the Apache Way." *National Geographic*, vol. 157, no. 2, February 1980, 262–271.

Rich, Adrienne. *Of Woman Born: Motherhood as Experience and Institution*. New York: W. W. Norton, 1986, p. 20.

Rigby, Cathy. *New Moon Magazine*, July/August 1995, 43–45.

"In the Ritual of Quinceañera, a Girl Is Queen for a Day." *NewYork Times*, 1 February 1996.

Rutter, Virginia Beane. *Woman Changing Woman: Feminine Psychology Re-Conceived Through Myth and Experience.* San Francisco: HarperSanFrancisco, 1993.

"Skintight Too Tight? Girls Team Fights Ban Over Shorts" *NewYork Times*, 10 January 1996.

Smith, Beverley Jean. "Raising a Resister" in Gilligan, et al., *Women, Girls, and Psychotherapy*, pp. 138 and 148.

Snyder, Zilpha Keatley. *Cat Running.* New York: Delacorte Press, 1994.

Steinem, Gloria. "Seeking Out the Missing Pieces of History." *New York Times*, 13 March 1992.

Stimpson, Catharine R. "Nancy Drew: 30s Sleuth, 90s Role Model." *NewYork Times*, 19 April 1993.

Thomasma, Kenneth. *Naya Nuki: Girl Who Ran.* Jackson, Wyoming: Grandview Publishing Co., 1983.

"White Weight." *Psychology Today*, September/October 1994, p. 9.

Wilford, John Noble. "Critics Batter Proof of an African Eve." *New York Times*, 19 May 1992.

Additional Resources for Girls and Women

■ ■ ■

Allende, Isabel. *Paula*. New York: HarperCollins, 1994.

American Association of University Women. *Shortchanging Girls, Shortchanging America* (1991); *How Schools Shortchange Girls* (1992).

Ashby, Ruth, and Deborah Gore Ohrn. Herstory: *Women Who Changed the World*. Penguin Viking, 1995.

Baum, Frank L. *The Wizard of Oz*. New York: Holt, Rinehart & Winston, 1982.

_____. *Ozma of Oz*. Chicago: Reilly & Lee Co., 1907.

Bender, Sue. *Everyday Sacred*. San Francisco: HarperSanFrancisco, 1995.

Bingham, Mindy, and Sandy Stryker. *Things Will Be Different for My Daughter: A Practical Guide to Building Her Self-Esteem and Self-Reliance from Infancy Through the Teen Years*. New York: Penguin Books, 1995.

Blais, Madeleine. *In These Girls Hope Is a Muscle: A True Story of Hoop Dreams and One Very Special Team*. New York: Warner Books, 1996.

Dove, Rita. *Mother Love: Poems*. New York: W. W. Norton & Co., 1995.

Erdrich, Louise. *The Blue Jay's Dance: A Birth Year*. New York: HarperCollins, 1995.

Gardner-Loulan, JoAnn, Bonnie Lopez, and Martha Quakenbush. *Period*. (In Spanish, *Periodo*.) Volcano, Calif.: Volcano Press, 1991.

Girl Power series of books published by Lerner Publications in Minneapolis. Written for girls ages 9 to 14, the series relies heavily on advice and reflections that girls themselves can offer.

Godfrey, Joline. *No More Frogs to Kiss: 99 Ways to Give Economic Power to Girls.* New York: HarperCollins, 1995.

Roessel, Monty. *Kinaaldá: A Navajo Girl Grows Up.* Minneapolis: Lerner Publications Co., 1993.

Hite, Shere. *The Hite Report On the Family: Growing Up Under the Patriarchy.* New York: Grove Press, 1994.

Hossfeld, Beth. *The Girls' Circle: A Facilitator's Guide to Providing Self-Esteem Circles for Early Adolescent Girls.* Beth Hossfeld, MFCC. 6 Knoll Lane, Ste. F, Mill Valley, CA, 94941. Tel. (415) 388-0644.

Lasky, Kathryn. *Double Trouble Squared.* New York: Harcourt, Brace, Jovanovich, 1991.

————. *Shadows in the Water.* New York: Harcourt, Brace, Jovanovich, 1992.

————. *A Voice in the Wind.* New York: Harcourt, Brace, Jovanovich, 1993.

Lawrence, Mary, ed. *Mother and Child: 100 Works of Art with Commentaries by 106 Distinguished People.* New York: Thomas Y. Crowell Co. 1975.

Mason, Bobbie Ann. *The Girl Sleuth: On the Trail of Nancy Drew, Judy Bolton, and Cherry Ames.* Athens, Georgia: University of Georgia Press, 1995.

Meador, Betty. *Inanna: Lady of Largest Heart* (unpublished).

Menstrual Health Foundation: Coming of Age Project. Tamara Slayton, 104 Petaluma Ave., Sebastopol, CA, 95472. Tel. (707) 829-2744.

Morrison, Toni. *Beloved.* New York: Alfred A. Knopf, 1987.

National Association for Girls and Women in Sports, 1900 Association Drive, Reston, VA, 72091.

Ryan, Joan. *Little Girls in Pretty Boxes: The Making and Breaking of Elite Gymnasts and Figure Skaters.* New York: Doubleday, 1995.

Seymour, Tryntje Van Ness. *The Gift of Changing Woman.* New York: Henry Holt & Co., 1993.

Sports Illustrated for Kids. New York: Time & Life Building, NY, 10020.

Strasser, Todd. *The Diving Bell.* New York: Scholastic Inc., 1992.

Tannen, Deborah. *You Just Don't Understand: Women and Men in Conversation.* New York: Ballantine, 1991.

Thompson, Ruth Plumly. *The Hungry Tiger of Oz.* New York: Ballantine, 1985.

————. *The Last King of Oz.* Chicago: Reilly & Lee Co., 1925.

————. *The Wishing Horse of Oz.* Chicago: Reilly & Lee Co., 1935.

Turecki, Stanley. *The Difficult Child.* New York: Bantam, 1985.

Wolf, Naomi. *The Beauty Myth: How Images of Beauty Are Used Against Women.* New York: William & Morrow Co., 1991.

Women of Our Time. Biographies of lives of twentieth-century women, covering a wide range of personalities in diverse fields for children and young adults. For example, *Dorothea Lange: Life Through the Camera; Eleanor Roosevelt: First Lady of the World;* and *Mother Teresa: Sister to the Poor.* New York: Viking Penguin.

The Women's Sport Foundation [Eisenhower Park, East Meadow, NY, 11554. Tel (800) 227-3988] has a junior membership program for girls. The $15 membership includes a quarterly newsletter written by women athletes.

Ask Virginia

If Celebrating Girls raised questions for you about nurturing and empowering your daughter, granddaughter, niece, goddaughter or any special girl in your life, please send them to Virginia Beane Rutter, c/o Conari Press. Virginia is collecting letters with such questions to be answered in a forthcoming book.

Virginia Beane Rutter
c/o Conari Press
2550 Ninth Street, Suite 101
Berkeley, California 94710

Conari Press, established in 1987, publishes books on topics ranging from spirituality and women's history to sexuality and personal growth. Our main goal is to publish quality books that will make a difference in people's lives—both how we feel about ourselves and how we relate to one another.

Our readers are our most important resource, and we value your input, suggestions, and ideas. We'd love to hear from you—after all, we are publishing books for you!

For a complete catalog or to get on our mailing list, please contact us at:

CONARI PRESS
2550 Ninth Street, Suite 101
Berkeley, California 94710

(800) 685-9595 ◆ Fax (510) 649-7190
e-mail: Conaripub@aol.com